DESTINY

_De_RAILED

How to Get Your Life Back on Track by Leveraging Your Past and Repurposing Your Pain into Power

JAMES FORTUNE

ELOHAI
INTERNATIONAL
PUBLISHING & MEDIA

Destiny Derailed

Published by ELOHAI International Publishing & Media
P.O. Box 64402
Virginia Beach, VA 23467
Elohailntl.com
Cover Design by Justin Foster
Jus10foster.com

Library of Congress Control Number: 2018908831
ISBN: 978-1-7324971-2-2

des·ti·ny de·railed

noun   *verb (past tense)*

when the events that will inevitably happen to a particular person or thing in the future (or a process) are obstructed and taken off course.

*D*edication

To everyone who's ever been knocked off course, experienced loss (of any kind), let themselves down and "failed," or thought that their situation closed the door to their destiny and disqualified them from God's promises, I dedicate this book to you.

My hope is that my journey will encourage and remind you that God loves you and is with you always.

- James

Acknowledgements

I always knew that God has placed a book on the inside of me. There was a story that needed to be told to remind people that no matter where you are or what you've done God's grace is greater than any mistake you may have made. I wasn't sure when He would release me to actually get it done, but I believed that when it was time, He would place the right people in my life at the right time to help me with this assignment. I've discovered that life is like a party. You invite a lot of people, some leave early, some stay all night, some laugh with you, some laugh at you, and some show up really late. But in the end, after the fun, there are only a few who stay to clean up the mess. And most of the time they aren't even the ones who made the mess. These people are your true friends in life. In 2014, I made a "mess" and I'm grateful to God for the few who stayed even after the mess was made.

I want to first thank my best friend Rhaquele who has supported and pushed me to keep going and to never stop believing in myself. There is no way I could have completed this book without your consistent love and support. You are the wind beneath my wings. I love you so much. To my children who are truly a gift from GOD to me: you have been so strong and supportive and your beautiful faces and smiles always push me to keep going forward and to be better. To my mom and sister, Sherry, for all the hours and hours of love and encouragement: we cried, laughed, and lifted one another up as we went through the most difficult season of our lives. I could never tell you how much I needed that. God blessed me with the best mom and sister in the world. I love you forever.

To my dad and Dr. Betty Fortune, thank you for taking me in and giving me words of wisdom and guidance throughout my life but especially over the last four years. I'm truly blessed to have a father like you. To my siblings DJ, Daryel, Danielle, Ayana, Will, and Latoya, thank you for your prayers and support. To Dr. Armond Brown, thank you not only for loving my mom as much as you do, but also for being there for me every and any time I asked you to. To Isaac Carree, man I could go on forever. You are truly one of a kind, man. I don't think I've ever cried with a grown man as much as we have cried together. Lol. There wasn't a day that went by that you didn't call to check on me and to pray with me. Loyalty is rare but you are the true definition of that word. I love you bro!

Tasha and Kenny Leonard I'm grateful to have you in my life. Thank you for always believing in me and supporting me. I thank GOD for your life and ministry. Bishop TD Jakes and Serita Jakes, I can't say enough about how much you meeting with us for over four hours changed my life forever. Thank you for taking the time to pour into me at a time when I needed it most. You may not have said everything I wanted to hear, but you said exactly what I needed to hear. I love you both. To Pastor Rhenel Johnson, thank you so much for loving me as your own son. I brag about you all the time and you were definitely a major reason that this book was completed. I love you. Nicole Heyward, thank you for everything you have done and continue to do to help with my ministry and career. You are a gift from GOD and a real joy to work with. You and your entire Creative Classic Agency team are first class. To Natasha T. Brown and ELOHAI International Publishing, I had never written a book before, and I didn't even know where to start, but after discussing my vision and ideas with you, you were able to guide me in the right direction. I'm forever grateful.

To all of my family and friends, even if I didn't say your name, I appreciate you and please understand that I needed you more than you realized it. To every supporter who sent me messages of love and support, I'm forever grateful. God knows what we need and when we need it, and your messages always seemed to come at just the right time. I would also like to thank these special individuals for being a blessing over the last four years, Pastor Keon, Real Talk Kim, Pastor Charles Jenkins, Pastor Welton Smith, Bishop William Murphy, Fred Hammond, Kirk Franklin, Gina Miller, Kerry Douglas, Cortez Nichols, Andre Roberson, Rev. Leslie Mathis, Ramone Harper, Anton Milton, Victor Mcray, Bishop Henry Fernandez, Apostle Travis and Stephanie Jennings, Pastor John and Aventer Gray, Pastor Jamal Bryant, Monica Brown, Shaunie O'neal, Alicia Malone, Monja Willis, Ty Morris, Nathalie Nicole, Chanita Foster, Marcus Dawson, Dr. Ivan Young, Malik Davis, and Justin Foster. Thank you all from the bottom of my heart.

Praise for Destiny Derailed

"James Fortune has been tasked with living out the unenviable calling of a gifted artist wrapped in flawed humanity. Oftentimes we like our gifts wrapped with the illusion of perfection. Yet the blood of Jesus is never more clearly viewed than when it is applied to the lives of those who are anointed-but have missed the mark in some way, shape, or form. Instead of hiding in the shadows, James most effectively ministers from the broken place and disarms devils by pointing the finger of responsibility at the one where it all began—himself. Let this work bless you and teach you the most valuable lesson of all: saying yes to God DOESN'T eliminate your frailties. It simply gives God permission to get glory out of them."

Pastor John Gray
Relentless Church

"This book is so full of healing. James literally poured out of a beautiful place of transparency. By the time you are done, you will be walking in complete healing! Forgiveness will set in, and shame will be completely gone. Your scars will be turned to stars. People with the worst past can indeed make the best futures."

Real Talk Kim
Church of The Harvest Fayetteville

"This book really proves that at its essence, a setback is nothing more than a set up for a comeback!"

Pastor Keion D. Henderson
The LightHouse Church of Houston

"Sometimes lessons learned are blessings earned and *Destiny Derailed* is a welcomed reminder of this concept. Whether you experience a private or public catastrophic decision, disastrous failure, or a heinous attack on your life, when you are a child of God, your greatest setback can be the precursor to your greatest comeback."

Pastor Charles Jenkins
Multi-Award Winning Artist
Pastor Fellowship Chicago

"I've been honored to walk out life with James not just when things were good, but even when things were at its worst. Loyalty is a lost art in society today, and I refused to walk away just because things got rough! *Destiny Derailed* is a glimpse of how tragedy, failure, honesty, and humility collided. I'm so glad to be able to witness when James' mistake derailed him, God's grace propelled him! Now he's walking in his destiny! To God be the glory!"

Isaac Carree
#1 Selling Gospel Artist & Author

"In our current dispensation, relevant and effective public ministry, almost always demands public testing and trial. I'm grateful to have had the privilege of being exposed to the redevelopment and elevation of James' testimony and ministry. What you are about to read, is an honest, responsible, transparent look into the personal life and headspace of one of our generation's most prolific writers and worshippers. My prayer is, that you will read, and listen, and hear God talking to you, and be encouraged to learn from, and then forget those things which are behind, and to reach for what's ahead, as you press your way towards destiny...in Jesus' name."

Bishop William Murphy, Lead Pastor
The Dream Center Church of Atlanta

Contents

Introduction

The bright red and blue police lights and the loud, overbearing two-way radios were a stark contrast to the peaceful Texas sky that covered the quiet community where we lived. My eyes itched, and I jerked my hand upward to scratch them, only to be reminded of the metal cuffs that constrained me at the wrists. A tall, white police officer walked out of my front door, with my two daughters and two sons behind him. Their heads were down, their night clothes were wrinkled, and their eyes squinted as to protect their pupils from the flashing lights. I could read the confusion and fear all over their faces. *Where's Dad?... Mom?...Why are we leaving?* Immediately, nausea overtook my upper body to the point of repulsion.

I wondered to myself, "What have I done?"

In that instant, I knew that my life would never be the same again. I sat in the back of that police car, attempting to replay the scenes from the previous four hours in my head. Yet I couldn't get past this question that kept scrolling through my mind—over and over again:

"How did I get here?"

This moment was the beginning of my life's biggest derailment.

The path leading up to that chilly night in Houston on October 23, 2014 wasn't perfect but my journey had been blessed. I never would have imagined that me—a preacher's kid from Richmond, Texas—would be in handcuffs and accused of assaulting my wife. Yet there I was. At the time, I couldn't understand the seriousness of what was happening. That my marriage was over. That I wouldn't see my children for several months, and my name and public reputation were about to hit a level equal to the scumof-the-earth. I wasn't quite ready to take responsibility for any of those consequences either. Media scrutiny, church scrutiny, family scrutiny—it hadn't yet hit me that this was about to be my life. I didn't know it in that moment, but so much was about to change so fast. I would lose my family. I would lose friends and fans. At times, I would even lose hope that the people who loved me, who knew me, people who I'd ministered to all over the world would now see me as a monster, as a man who beat his wife. I feared that I'd lose the respect of men like Bishop T.D. Jakes of The Potter's House, who believed in me. I didn't know, sitting in the back of that police cruiser, that my guilt would prompt me to take a 240-mile drive from Houston to Dallas to visit Bishop Jakes face-to-face. I did not yet realize that he would hold back no truth when he informed me that I'd just become the face of the abuser for domestic violence survivors everywhere. I'd kick myself over and over again, feeling like I had betrayed him and the thousands of women that I had recently ministered to at the Woman Thou Art Loosed conference. All of this hadn't hit me in those lonely, uncertain moments while I was awaiting the awful trip to the local police station. As my children walked across the lawn—unaware that their daddy sat in the back of that car, all I could think about was, "Where are they taking my kids and when can I get them back?"

As a child, I would've bet my mom's rent money that my future would be set by some type of fame and stardom from football or baseball. I was into Little League sports and *all* I wanted to do was throw or catch a ball. By the time I entered middle school, I had begun writing poetry and rhymes in my spare time, and I started playing the drums, but my true musical gift hadn't been awakened yet. My father was a pastor, and he required me to be involved in ministry. There were no football or baseball teams at Rock of Salvation Church, so when it came time for me to pick a ministry and take up the mantle as a PK, my best and most entertaining option seemed like the youth choir. I joined, and soon it sparked a love for music in me, one that I never knew was there. The way that lyrics connected with melodies and beats and could make people dance, laugh, cry, shout, and praise was something that I couldn't let go of once I held it. As soon as I made that discovery, my life was never the same. I collided with my destiny path and suddenly the rhymes and poems that I was writing had purpose.

I started performing with a group of kids who also attended my church around the Houston, Texas area, and we developed a buzz. People started to know me as an up-and-coming gospel artist. I enjoyed music ministry and as I grew older into my late teens, the performance engagements picked up for me. I met my wife in my early twenties after returning to Houston from a short stint at Cal State. She was also a singer, so we began to perform together. After a few years of doing ministry together, we married and soon had babies—three, one after another.

I was living my dream. I worked odd jobs at various places, including an insurance and a water company, but my passion was music. With church and the local performance scene, we stayed busy. I was happy—eventually one song gained a little popularity, and then another hit big (I'll share more details later). Then came the Grammy nominations, Stellar Awards, and, just like that (or least that is how it felt) I had a music career, a family, fans, hit songs, and I was living my ministry dream—all for God's glory.

Then, one blow after another attempted to take me out. "Life" happened and it all came to a halt on October 23, 2014. That was the night that I was forever changed. One bad decision, an equally bad reaction, then just like a roller coaster at an amusement park, everything suddenly spiraled downward until the life I was living was just a slight resemblance of the life God and I had designed together for so many years. This was the beginning of a *Destiny Derailed,* and I know I'm not alone. Behind the lights, cameras, big smiles, Instagram stories, and public appearances, we all experience difficult trials. I wasn't used to failure (or what I deemed to be failure at the time), so I was literally shell shocked into mental, emotional, and physical uncharted territory. I have a feeling that you've found yourself there too.

Can you recall a time when everything was going well for you, and then, out of nowhere, your destiny was derailed? Maybe it was an illness, bankruptcy, accident, tragedy, divorce, or unemployment. Whatever hit you was an expected, catastrophic event, or some series of traumas, that took the destined life that you thought was yours—or at least tried. You got derailed.

That's what happened to me. *Derailment... off track. Course interrupted.*

Little-by-little, it seemed that the life I'd worked so hard for, and the destiny I sacrificed and prayed for, slipped through my fingers much faster than it took to build. At this point in their story, most people begin to question life, God Himself, or His plans. We ask, "Is it possible to get it all back—to rebuild?" "How can things ever be like they were?" "How will I ever dig myself out of this hole?" and "Everything seemed so perfect before." These were the thoughts that I had. Over and over, I meditated on these questions and attempted to recreate the past or construct the future. I held on so tightly to the pain and discouragement that, at times, I missed what God was doing. Everything seemed so perfect before.

Seemed perfect. In reality, though, I've learned that the destiny derailments that we experience are typically the culmination of a series of events that have been brewing behind the scenes for a long time—arguments, anger, resentment, cutting corners, slack, ungratefulness, selfishness—something. Perhaps we're simply speeding through life too fast, our motives are impure, or our perspective on life as a whole or a specific situation is out of whack. When we consider the negative ingredients that reside below the surface, derailment is often inevitable. It's just like the new homeowners who close on a house on Thursday only to experience a basement flood on Saturday. With that flood, they uncover a deeper issue—mold within the drywall and flooring. The mold had been there under the surface of that home the entire time. The previous owners may have even known about this issue and intentionally didn't disclose it. But as that rising water receded, what was once hidden is now obvious. Eventually, these new home owners would inevitably uncover that mold. It couldn't hide forever.

The perfect set of circumstances will always reveal issues that have been hidden by superficial cover ups. This is true not only for moldy houses, but relationships with unhealthy partners, children who deal with untreated pain, symptoms of sickness that we don't see the doctor for, or money that we never learn how to manage.

These below-the-surface, untreated issues often cause many of the destiny derailments that we experience in life. The mold that's hiding in our walls is always going to show itself eventually. It's just a matter of when.

After this book's title came to me, I began to research famous train derailments in our country and world history. I learned that in August of 1904, a train accident in Colorado claimed ninety-six lives. The wreck was caused by a flash flood which crashed into wooden train tracks, causing the vehicle to lose its bearings and veer off track. On November 2, 1918, a five-car train wreck happened in New York, and it's still considered the worst in that city's history. As the train approached the Malbone Street tunnel in Brooklyn, it hit a deadly curb, jumped the tracks, and plunged into a concrete partition between the north and south bound tracks. Ninety-seven people were killed on the spot and five additional people later succumbed to their injuries. The cause of this accident was speed. Similarly, On September 6, 1943, seventy-nine passengers died instantly when a train car on The Congressional Limited caught fire outside of Philadelphia causing the train to flip off of its tracks. In these three historic derailments, there were different reasons that caused the crashes—speed and recklessness, a storm, and a fire.

Just like a *Destiny Derailed,* there can be various causes of train derailments. So reading these historic accounts made me wonder… "James, what caused your derailment?"

Necessary Questions

Today, I pose that same question to you. Have you sat down to figure out why your destiny was derailed? Do you have bottled-up emotions that need to be sorted through? Are your relationships healthy or are there people who have caused your train to travel off course? If you were to be hit with the elements—fire, water, wind—something that shook things up in your life, would your train stay on course or would it be derailed? How about the people who are around you? Are your relationships built on a firm foundation? Are you built on a firm foundation? How's your faith? How's your devotion time with God? How is your belief in yourself? Have you dealt with the hurt from the past, the resentment and bitterness that crept in from the broken promises and dead-end relationships that you have encountered? Have you forgiven your father, your mother? These are hard, but necessary questions, to face. Our culture has grown so accustomed to sweeping things under the rug, to painting over mold, and putting makeup over bruises that we rarely spend time with self and time with God, and time with the loved ones in our lives truly unmasking the issues and healing from the pain. When we fail at this, we agree to ride on a train that is destined to derail.

As I spent time healing following that October night, I found myself in various forms of therapy—including group therapy with several men who had also assaulted their wives or girlfriends. Different circumstances had led each of us to the same place and one moment in time where we could choose healing and to get back on track after derailment or continue making excuses for ourselves. In this book, I'm going to push you to search your soul and figure out why. Why was your *Destiny Derailed* and how will you get back on God's intended course for you? Many people give up on themselves and give up on God when something terrible happens. They reason: "A god who is loving and merciful and who sees everything wouldn't possibly allow this to happen, therefore there must not be a god." Too often, we, as humans, create this idol of a god, who we say shouldn't allow this or that, and then we reject the One True God. Many atheists and agnostics are born from situations like these. The truth is that the Bible (God's divinely inspired Word) never tells us that life will be easy or that we won't experience hard times. In fact, it shows us just the opposite. The most perfect person in the world—Jesus Christ—God Himself, experienced betrayal, torture, abandonment, all at the hands of people whom He had served and ministered to for three years.

He experienced the most horrific act in world history, and yet the story didn't end there. The crucifixion of Christ was just a *Destiny Derailed.* His real destiny was resurrection. Your real destiny is resurrection too.

It's human nature to pay close attention to what is happening in our individual lives, rather than to consider what is happening in the entire universe, especially in the days to come. It's impossible for us to know the future unless God reveals it to us. God's job is to know and pre-construct our futures. He knows when we get off track and when we have steered off of our destiny paths. Even when He seems far away, He is right there. When we give up, write God off as One who doesn't understand or care, or lose faith that life can change, we end up **living** (and establishing a house and home) in a place that should have been a temporary train stop. The name of this book is called *Destiny Derailed* and not *Derailed Destination,* because the derailment is not a permanent place of residence. The Bible tells us that God met our end before our beginning (Isa. 46:10); He knew us before we were formed in our mother's womb (Jer. 1:5), and so that tells us that the hard times we face are not a surprise to Him. He can handle them; and since we made it through, we can handle these situations too. There's a purpose for the derailments, and my hope and prayer is that this book will help you discover that. It rains on the just and the unjust (Matt. 5:45). That means that both good and bad people will experience storms. God wants you to know exactly how to handle them.

More important than wondering, "Why did this happen?" are your answers to, "What's next?" and "What's now?"

As God ministered me back on track following my life's greatest setback, He showed me the various underlying issues that had led to my crash. Then, He took me on a journey of rehabilitation, accountability, learning to love myself, and trusting Him. God showed me that derailments often happen to prevent an even worse accident from occurring. As I examined my life at that time—the abuse, the root causes of that abuse, and the anger that had accumulated from years of untreated issues, I could only imagine how worse my situation might have become had my destiny not been derailed. See, not all derailments end in death, and God promises to make all things work together for our good (Rom. 8:28). Some derailments, even when we consider train derailments, are simply purposeful detours—such was the case in March of 2016 when an Amtrak operator in rural Kansas made an executive decision to apply the emergency brakes on the train after he noticed a significant bend in the tracks ahead. This brave and courageous move saved the lives of the 140 passengers on board. This is how God treats His children.

He will allow or often cause a derailment in our destinies when there is danger ahead. Recognizing the imminent danger (and God's protection) after the fact takes a perspective shift and an ability to trust God's Word for what it says. I have watched the derailments in my life serve as wilderness moments when I learned and grew—moments right before God's next mountaintop experiences for my life. I am not saying that we must be derailed in order to experience destiny, but sometimes, our own choices make derailment the best option in the long run. Sometimes, derailments are simply divine detours to protect our destinies so that God can receive the glory (See John Chapter 11).

A *Destiny Derailed* is when a person gets off course, misaligned, and off track due to a circumstance or situation (or several situations). The purpose of this book is to help you shift your perspective so that God may orchestrate your life's greatest comeback.

When derailments occur, the focus is automatically on what has been lost. However, in the midst of my questioning if I could ever recoup what was taken from me, God changed the subject and told me that He would redeem the time, not necessarily the material things. There will often be casualties in derailments. God prunes what can grow and removes what can't. God doesn't always restore material possessions or people who succumbed to the derailments in our lives, because He replaces those people and things with better matches for the future, for our destiny. I know that many people who have dealt or are dealing with divorce or the loss of relationship, like I have, are asking the question, "How do I get the time back that I spent with that person?" If that is you, just realize that the *how* isn't important. Joel 2:25 promises us that God will redeem the time. The Lord also revealed to me that our focus after a derailment does not need to be about how to get the past back, because God wants to do a new thing with a new and improved you. That means you may not get back what you lost. He wants you to leave the past where it is and focus on Him so that you don't miss the new thing that He is doing in your future.

Have you ever seen one of those shows on HGTV where a couple gets a complete home makeover? Think of a restored house, or a piece of furniture; often you can't tell that it was ever an old, beat-up object, because through that restoration process, the builder created something totally new—with fresh materials that are more modern and can last longer.

Isaiah 43:19 tells us, *"Behold, I will do a new thing, now it shall spring forth; Shall you not know it? I will even make a road in the wilderness And rivers in the desert."*

The prophet Job in the Old Testament is an example of this. The Lord lifted his hedge of protection and Satan was allowed to destroy his family and all of his possessions. Talk about *Destiny Derailed!* Job found himself pleading his case with his friends in hopes of finding one friend who'd encourage him. That didn't happen, however, Job stayed faithful. He trusted God, and eventually the Lord restored him—not by bringing his children and former possessions back to life, but by giving him a new life—additional children, cattle, land, and wealth. God redeemed Job's time by giving him double! The revelation that God wants to redeem the time and provide something new was exciting to me. As I continue to live a life surrendered to God, and as He continues to rebuild me after my life's greatest setback, I have great hope. The *Destiny Derailed* that I experienced did not kill me nor did it stop God's plans for my life. My destiny did not die in that derailment either, and neither did yours.

Job experienced the loss of many people he knew and the very life that he had grown accustomed to. He lost his credibility and stature in society. His relationships became rocky and his self-esteem hit an all-time low. It seemed like he'd lost everything, but in the end, we see that he did not lose the most valuable thing—God's love and favor. No matter how much the devil tested him, how much Job had to give up and the various people and possessions to which he had to say "goodbye" to, God never ever said "goodbye" to Job. Like most of us in a situation like that, Job began to question God, and God finally spoke to him. He corrected Job and his friends' faulty thinking and began the best comeback plan ever.

If you're ready to experience a transformational journey, where God redeems your time and sets you back on the path toward destiny, let's go. Let's take this ride of restoration. God is ready to put you back on track, just like He did with Job and just like he did with me. I know what it's like to be derailed from a destiny, and my passion is to help all those who come in contact with me and this book to experience what God has for you—regardless of what you've been through. As an artist, I've always created songs that encourage and help people get through some of their most difficult, unimaginable seasons of adversity. Today my friend, that's my prayer for you as you turn the pages of this book. I pray that these words help you to bounce back, get back on track, and experience a destiny that is magnificent and indescribable.

Chapter 1: *I Trust You*

In 1999, I returned home to Houston after attending California State Northridge for a year and a half. The atmosphere at CSU was completely different from what I was used to and not conducive to my dream of becoming a successful gospel singer. I rarely saw any black faces, and it was a major culture shock, to say the least. I left college and decided to pursue my dream of becoming a gospel singer full time.

When I arrived back to Houston, I hit the ground running working in ministry at my dad's church, Rock of Salvation, with his youth choir as an evangelist and minister. I spent much of my free time with other members of my church and group sharing Jesus Christ and writing music. I and the other young adults at church would sing and evangelize to people in Sharpstown Mall. (If you're from Houston you definitely remember that place.) Then, once we ministered through song and the Word, we would invite people back to the church where I taught Bible study each Monday night. While I no longer attended a formal university, God thrust me into His very own school of ministry where witnessing and performing were my first-year course load. During this time, I developed a boldness for telling people about Jesus, and the music became an entryway to win souls for Christ. Over time, however, God used my entire life to raise me in the faith and I lived the very lyrics I wrote. I needed God desperately, and I would call upon Him in dark hours. He would minister comforting words to me that brought me through, and I would transform those words into songs that ministered to others. Over the next few years, success and suffering would teach me many lessons that have equipped me for ministry. Have you ever thought about how your life's purpose makes perfect sense? One of the ways that I learned to trust God was through reflection—I could see God's hand in my life even in the hard times. I believe that there is a thread of God throughout our lives even before we realize it or formally accept the Lord as our Savior. The thread can be traced from our childhood through the point when we have stepped into purpose. Not only that, I saw how God repurposed my painful moments into more positive experiences through my music ministry. It's true that nothing is wasted in the kingdom of God. Even the moments that we'd rather forget and stuff in a closet out of public sight are tools that can be used to glorify God.

Speaking of God-threads, I once heard someone say that God will give us a glimpse of destiny before allowing us to walk fully into it. Biblically speaking, this idea could be affirmed by looking at the story of Joseph, for instance. In Genesis Chapter 37, Joseph was just seventeen-years-old. His father, Israel, (Jacob) loved him more than his other sons, since he had been born to Jacob in his old age. This chapter explains two dreams that Joseph had which caused his destiny to be derailed. In the first dream, Joseph told his brothers, "We were binding sheaves of grain out in the field when suddenly my sheaf rose and stood upright, while your sheaves gathered around mine and bowed down to it." Immediately, his brothers interpreted this dream to mean that Joseph would be the ruler over them. Joseph's second dream truly caused trouble for the young man. "Then he had another dream, and he told them again. "Listen," he said, "I had another dream, and this time the sun and moon and eleven stars were bowing down to me." Joseph's father and brothers essentially rebuked Joseph, but his brothers wanted to get rid of him. Although Joseph's life took a terrible turn for the worse when he was thrown into a pit and sold into slavery, through his story, we see God constantly with him. Joseph was favored while in the pit, in prison, and in the palace. A *Destiny Derailed* does not mean that the destiny is terminated. The very definition of the word "destiny" insinuates that it is bound to happen. In Joseph's life, we see God—the promise keeper—bringing his dream, his destiny, to pass, despite his derailments. This is the nature of our God. Years later, when Joseph was reunited with his brothers as he provided for them during a great famine he said, "You intended to harm me, but God intended it for good to accomplish what is now being done, the saving of many lives" (Gen. 50:20). Through Joseph's story, we can see that regardless of the path that we walk or how derailed we become, God can and will ensure that we reach the destination.

Let's take a look at another story in the Bible when God revealed a glimpse of the destiny that was to come. You've heard the story of King David in the Old Testament, right? He was anointed as king as a young shepherd boy. He didn't look like a typical choice for king. David was younger, smaller, and less experienced in the natural than any of his other brothers. However, God wanted to do something new in the lives of His chosen people. David's story demonstrates that we don't have to be qualified to be called to do something great. We don't even have to look the part. We don't have to be the biggest, the most experienced, or the obvious choice of people. In fact, being called by God is the only qualification required to go from a young, inexperienced shepherd boy to the greatest king next to the Messiah Himself. God positioned David in King Saul's palace, and had him play the harp for the king to soothe the tormenting spirit that disturbed him day in and day out. David was in the right position when the giant Goliath came about chastising God's people.

The confidence that David developed tending sheep and fighting off wild animals for years ensured him that he could also put an end to Goliath. God gave David a glimpse of his future and the victory that he would have against Goliath. While David tended his father's sheep and kept them safe from wild animals during the night hours, David was actually practicing the same skills that would make him confident enough to challenge and defeat the giant Goliath. As a shepherd, he didn't know that one day he would become a warrior. He simply served in the place where he was located. David was faithful, and eventually with those same skills, he became a great warrior and king whose bloodline would birth Jesus. It's true that some of life's greatest derailments can actually propel us into purpose.

In 2005, I experienced the first major blow to my life. I didn't like it at the time. I probably even complained and I definitely would not have chosen this road for myself, however, in hindsight, I can admit that if it were not for this situation, I probably wouldn't be the man that I am today. Nor would I be prepared for what I would experience years later. At the time, I was young, married, and had two young children. I worked in the mailroom of an insurance company by day, but at nights and on weekends, I performed with my band, James Fortune & FIYA, and also led the youth choirs at two local churches. Despite the opportunities to minister, both I and many of my group members began to grow frustrated with the climate of gospel music in our region, Houston, Texas. I knew that we couldn't expect overnight fame and success, that it took hard work, so we put in hours upon hours in the studio and performed wherever we could. We made songs that seemed and sounded like hits—songs that people loved and they told us so. But no matter how hard we worked and how many hours we put in, it seemed like nothing would stick. Radio stations didn't accept our sound.

I had been working on my demo for a while and yet it wasn't happening for me. I had several meetings with labels in Houston, but no one really believed in me or wanted to give the group's music an opportunity. I began to question if I should just give up and do something else. I knew that working in a mailroom wasn't my calling, but it provided steady pay without the disappointment that seemed to be attached to pursuing gospel music full time. I was growing very discouraged, to say the least, and I yearned for our big break. Despite growing a fan base, performing regularly, serving at churches, and being well-known in Houston, it was a disheartening process of blessings followed by rejection.

We desperately wanted to break into the national circuit, yet we stayed just below the radar, unable to hit it big or get the attention of music executives who wanted to truly help us soar higher than this invisible plateau. It felt like we had reached our ceiling, yet my desire to pursue music wouldn't let me quit. I knew that we had what it took and that our music was just as encouraging and well-arranged as other gospel and contemporary Christian artists that were on the scene. After a while, the singers that were in the group decided to leave, because we weren't successful at getting an album deal. One-by-one the group diminished, until the only people who remained were me, my sister, my wife, and one friend. I sat down one day, fed up to my ears in hopelessness, and God started to speak the following words into my spirit:

Though you've been hurt by someone
And you feel your smile is gone
No one can understand your tears
Or what you've been through just to make it through
The pain that you felt hurt so deep inside
And you often ask yourself why

But you survived, you survived
All the pains that you went through
But Jehovah brought you through
You survived, you survived it all

These words became the lyrics to my first mainstream hit, "You Survived."

Have you ever experienced a moment when you knew that something magical was happening? As these words poured out of my soul and onto the piece of paper that I was writing on, I knew that there was something different about this song. It was birthed from a place of uncertainty, a place of disappointment, yet it was a place of divine intervention. I could feel the presence of God in that moment. I recorded the song immediately and put it in the hands of my friend, Anthony Valery, who worked at Gospel 1590 KYOK AM in Houston. The song began to get local airplay and one day another radio announcer, Charles Hudson on KTSU, was playing the song. A record executive by the name of Kerry Douglas happened to hear it and called the radio station to find out who the artist was, and he immediately offered me a record deal based on that one song. Kerry and I established a great business relationship, and my ministry engagements soon increased as "You Survived" gained traction throughout the area gospel circuit.

On August 23, 2005, one of the most devastating storms in the country, Hurricane Katrina, hit my hometown. This was the third strongest hurricane ever to impact the U.S. at the time—the final death toll was over 1,800 people from Louisiana to Mississippi, and grave images of displaced African-Americans hijacked television broadcasts for weeks. The country's criticism of President George W. Bush defined that time, and artists such as Lil Wayne protested against the country's slow response to provide aid to victims. I was a rising national act, and "You Survived" caught a lot of traction by then. That song became a popular soundtrack to the unfortunate circumstances and aftermath of Hurricane Katrina. I received so many kind, emotional messages from survivors, DJs, and others that the song was a blessing to Katrina survivors—it provided hope and the lyrics spoke to the grief and pain that so many people were going through in such scary times. It renewed a sense of hope that they would need to get through what they were facing:

By the grace of GOD
You made it through
With His strength and power
He gave to you
In spite of all
You can smile again
You can hold your head up high
You Survived.

One day, not too long afterwards, while I was at work, I received a call from Kerry informing me that he had received an offer for me to join the twenty-five city, One Church Tour. Kurt Carr was headlining, and other popular artists were performing on tour as well, including Smokie Norful, VaShawn Mitchell, and Rizen. I quit my job in the mail room immediately and left home to tour the country. This was my big break. Finally, it was happening. Everyone involved in my career at the time was ecstatic. We were going to make the most out of this one shot.

The organizers gave me five minutes on stage every night, and I performed "You Survived." It was amazing to see how I was virtually an unknown artist when the announcers introduced me to the stage—then inevitably each crowd went crazy once the track began to play. Once my five minutes were up, I went to my merchandise table and sold dozens of CDs. Every night on tour was virtually the same routine—no one knew my name once I hit the stage. I stepped before the crowd, the track began to play, the crowd went wild, and everyone who I could see sang along with me. It was the grace of God that opened that door for me. It was like a movie. If you've watched biopics of groups like The Temptations, Tina Turner, Ray Charles, or The Jackson Five, you can imagine the way I felt traveling the country alongside major artists and witnessing my song move crowds. In my heart, I knew that this was *IT!*

Some of the most rewarding moments came as we traveled the country to different hotels and I would meet various people who had been displaced by Hurricane Katrina. Their homes were destroyed by the storm and their lives were ripped apart, but over and over, time and time again, many people expressed that "You Survived" provided encouragement and hope during those difficult times. During the One Church Tour, my faith increased as it pertained to my destiny in music. It was my first time traveling outside of my local area ministering music, professionally, for God, and it felt amazing. I never wanted this feeling to end. I never wanted the tour to end either! No, I was not quite yet at the level of the other more experienced artists on the tour, but God allowed me to get a glimpse of my future. I peeped into the window of my destiny, and while I was on the road I hadn't yet realized it was just a sneak peek. I had more lessons to learn. Just like Joseph after his dream and David after he was anointed, it was not quite my time to step into that destiny just yet. After the tour was over, I returned to business as usual. This is when my life took an unexpected turn and things got real interesting.

Unexpected Turns

I didn't make much money at all on that tour. In fact, I didn't get paid virtually anything, besides a $500 stipend for my hotel room each week and whatever I sold in merchandise. It was a promotional experience for both myself and VaShawn Mitchell, who was also a new artist at the time. Despite the lack of money, I was grateful to be on the tour. It was my dream and an opportunity to promote my first album. The little money I earned had to support me, two children, and my wife who was pregnant with our third child at the time. But the sacrifice was worth it. I felt like this was my shot, and I just knew that when we came off of the road, things would be poppin'. Much to my disappointment, they weren't.

When the tour was over after two and a half months, I came back home to no job and no money. I'd quit my job, when in reality perhaps I should have taken a leave of absence. I didn't think further into the future prior to accepting the tour gig, because I believed what I saw on TV. I thought that once I got home, things would be good. In my dreams, I saw bigger record deals, more tour dates, and money flowing into my bank account faster than I needed it. I expected the phone to be jumping and the paychecks to be piling up. I thought that I'd be booked and every gospel promoter, church pastor, and event planner would want me to be on their lineups. I'd heard so many stories and I believed that my story would end the same way... I believed that I would experience the same sudden turnaround in my career after the tour. Surely I'd go from a no-name musician to a gospel music star, right? However, what we experienced was the total opposite. My life wasn't peaches and cream after that first tour. I had traveled the country ministering to people who were displaced because of the hurricane and here I was facing the same sudden fate. It didn't take long for us to get underwater in bills and expenses. My wife and I were renting a home. Without steady jobs, we could no longer pay anything. Soon the inevitable happened; we received an eviction notice and were put out of our place.

The average person would swallow their pride and seek help at this point. It would have been perfectly understandable, especially with the children and newborn baby on the way. For me, that was not an option. I was extremely prideful. I grew up with a pastor as a father and was taught that it wasn't good for a man to fail in taking care of his family. To me, saving face and maintaining public perception that I was successful was more important than asking for and accepting help. Just imagine how you'd feel after just coming off of tour, having a hot song in heavy rotation on the radio, and being the leader and "provider" of a growing family with a new baby on the way. I knew that God would take care of us. I constantly thought, "What's the worst that could happen?" I instructed my wife not to tell anyone what we were going through. I assured her that we would be good—but that we shouldn't tell anyone what was going on. It's a decision that I would later regret, but I thought that the humiliation of being a broke, gospel music so-called star was far worse than actually asking for help.

Once we were evicted, my family had to sleep in motels when we could afford the daily rates. Sometimes, we had enough for a week at a time, but those days were short-lived. We couldn't afford that for too long, and when our money ran out, we slept in our car—my wife and I in the front seats, and our two oldest children in the back. For seven months, we had no stable place to live—we slept in the car and hotel rooms. I often wondered how this happened. The memories of performing on stage in front of thousands of fans were at the forefront of my mind; the tour seemed like it was just yesterday, like no time had passed. I often envisioned that things were better. That I was on tour, with more than enough for my family, that my family and I could afford the luxuries that others enjoyed. I wondered when our lives would change. No one knew the truth—not even our church. The stress of not knowing where we would live or how long I would be able to feed my family took an emotional toll on me, and I believe that this may have been the beginning roots of anger that would later resurface.

Despite being a bit prideful, I was not lazy. I searched for jobs and a way to provide for my family. I couldn't seem to find a full-time job that could provide for all of our needs. I was volunteering and working part time at a church, but I really wasn't making a lot of money. My wife was laid off from her job, and things seemed to get more difficult by the day. I wondered, "How did we get here? How am I, James Fortune, whose song is playing on the radio right now sleeping in my car?"

As the Proverb tells us, pride comes before destruction and a haughty spirit before a fall. Being homeless took a toll on every aspect of my life—it was an emotional battle between me and the enemy. He spoon-fed me lies, and I began questioning everything from my self-worth, to my purpose, to God's plan for my life, and my decision to quit my job and perform on the One Church Tour. Of course being alone with my thoughts and despair for such a long time was unhealthy. I assumed that because I was enduring a hard time, I had made the wrong decision by leaving my stable, but dead-end job and chasing my dream and touring. Of course, this too was a lie. Living in this vulnerable state took a toll on my faith which then made me lose perspective of the big picture. Sometimes the paths to our dreams are not easy. Sometimes, it will require sleeping in cars, hotel rooms, having less than we would want. Not having the support of my family (due to my own pride and embarrassment) made things worse. I hit the lowest point in my life—a point so far down that my own human ability couldn't pull me up.

In King David fashion (when he was hiding in the wilderness from his own son—while penning Psalms) I began to pour out my heart to God. Desperation and a dependency on Him brought me to my knees. I humbled myself before God and prayed like never before. I surrendered. There was no more pride. Never mind the embarrassment. I needed a breakthrough, and there was only one being who could help me through this. One night, in a motel room, as I gazed at my pregnant wife and beautiful children as they slept and beat myself up because they deserved none of this, I began to question Him. Many people would argue that we shouldn't question God, but I've learned that God doesn't mind questions at all. In fact, in our moments of questioning, He will surely answer. He loves to answer. An overwhelming heaviness and unbearable depression caused the tears to fall like never before. I said, "God I don't really understand why I'm going through this. I love you and I love your people. I'm doing what you called me to do. I'm doing ministry, and I'm using the gifts that you have given to me. Why is this happening? What do I do to make it right?"

He interrupted me, "James, if you can trust me now while you're in this situation, even though you don't understand why I'm doing what I'm doing, you will experience something you never have before—I'm getting ready to do something in your life, and if I explained it to you, you would not believe it."

In my spirit, I knew that God had answered me. He heard my cries and He responded. However, it was still really hard to trust Him when all I could see was darkness in front of and around me. I didn't really know what was happening, but despite what I felt, I began to say, "God, I trust you. Even if I can't see you, I trust you, even though I can't see you, God I trust you." When you don't know what to say or do, repeating those Bible-based affirmations to yourself will help you become convinced that everything will be alright. I started writing the words to the song "I Trust You" that night. The words flowed to me so effortlessly, because they were words that God ministered directly to my soul. That night in that hotel room with God, His words to me, and my response to Him, gave me the assurance that I desperately needed at the time. "I Trust You" became my personal anthem to pull myself through that hard time of homelessness and poverty—a time when I hid my truth from society while fighting to change my narrative.

That same week, I taught the song to my group. Once we had a solid recording of it, I sent the track to the producers, and we put it on the album we were working on entitled *Transformation*. I remember when we were first trying to get "I Trust You" placed in radio rotation and no one really wanted to play it. I was not a well-known artist, and quite frankly, the stations thought they were taking a "risk" when it came to me. Sure, I had one song that did really well. People knew "I Survived", but they really didn't know me. I suffered from a lack of brand identity. The success of my first song made people think that I was a one-hit wonder according to the local and national gospel music radio executives. They said "I Trust You" sounded too much like a Kirk Franklin song. It was hard. Kerry Douglas and I would go around to radio stations. The radio programmers enjoyed meeting me, but they really weren't feeling the record. Despite the closed doors that we continued to face, I remained faithful and committed to getting the song out. I knew that God had given it to me. The Holy Spirit wrote those words, and I was just a vessel. I was sure of it and confident, although a little discouraged, that it would soon pick up traction. Why would God give me something only to allow it to be a failure? I had no choice but to believe. My back was against the wall. My family barely had meals on our table, my new baby was due in a matter of weeks, and my family still didn't have a permanent address. If this didn't work, I didn't know what would. I felt in my heart that "I Trust You" was God's grace and provision that would take us to our next place after being, what my friend Tasha Cobbs calls, "Gracefully Broken." God was there with me and my family. I knew that I just needed to hold on.

Eventually, a few stations started playing it, and at the same time, I kept ministering it live. Those live moments on the stage were incredible. The way that song literally shook and moved people was like watching magic. I knew that we were touching people who were dealing with similar issues that I was—they were having difficulty trusting God, but knew that they needed to live by faith. Even while the song was not receiving much airplay, it was a wrap when we'd minister it live. I saw the momentum that I had with live audiences and I continued to perform "I Trust You" over and over, wherever I could get a mic and a stage. After performances, the lines at my merchandise table were wrapped around the corner. Everyone who heard that song wanted it. A buzz began to grow. Radio stations started playing it repeatedly. Then, it started moving up the charts. At the time, there was a huge song out—"Never Would Have Made It" by Marvin Sapp, and it was number one on the gospel charts. On August 30, 2008, "I Trust You" peaked at #1 and remained in that position for several weeks. After replacing Marvin's song, it set the all-time record for consecutive weeks on the Billboard charts as a #1 song for twenty-nine weeks in a row, which is approximately seven months—the same amount of time that my family and I were homeless. God told me that if I trust Him, He would do something that I would never believe. To have a song go #1 is amazing, and He was right. I never would have imagined that I'd see that type of success after sleeping in my car with my wife and babies just weeks before. It was a dream to say the least, especially for a new artist. Secular stations began to play the song and it changed everything. As the writer and artist of "I Trust You," I was living a real dream. God opened so many doors. That song changed my life and pushed me to international status.

As "I Trust You" climbed the charts, I often fell into deep reflection and gratitude. I wasn't happy about being homeless, but I was grateful to witness God move so miraculously in my life. After the biggest derailment of my life at the time, there I was experiencing the greatest victory and this time, it happened quickly. There was always a mountain after the valley and a river beyond the dessert. The downs that I experienced enabled me to appreciate the incredible moment so much more. With every opportunity to minister, every chance that my wife and I could pay a bill, and witnessing my baby girl's birth in the midst of this season are times that I will never forget. To trust God was our only choice. He set my life up in such a way that I would proclaim that truth from coast-to-coast in a way that would inspire all who needed to hear it. We all needed to be reminded that we could trust God no matter what our natural circumstances look like. To this day, that song still impacts people.

Following the release of "I Trust You," in the same year, I witnessed my dreams come true in various ways. I performed on TBN (which was on my performance bucket list); The Celebration of Gospel, (another dream); Bobby Jones Gospel, (I had been watching that show since I was a child), and I performed at the Stellar Gospel Music Awards. I did all of that in a twelve-month period. I remember literally sitting down one day thinking,

Oh my God. This is nobody but God. I remember how low I was when He gave me that song, and to see how He is using the same song that He gave to me when I was in this desperate place of feeling like I was a failure as a father and a husband. Now it is blessing so many people all over the world. I can see now why He allowed me to go through that season, because that was the only way that this song could have come out of me. It's important to note that I never really dealt with the emotional and psychological trauma that this situation caused me. This is going to be important a little later.

Enduring seven months of homelessness and desperation was probably one of few circumstances that could have brought that song out of me. I could not have written it while I was prospering with everything going well and money in the bank account. I felt in my spirit that God needed to allow me to go through this place of persecution, despair, and adversity in order to pull that out of me—so that others could be blessed. It was amazing as an artist to even see how stations refused to play it at first. Then, it went on to being the most played song for the greater part of a year. To this day, over ten years later, I can go anywhere and sing "I Trust You," and it will still have the same powerful impact. The perfectly curated lives that we post on social media often cannot produce the anointing that God destined for us. It often takes grit and grime, tears, anger, sadness, and uncertainty. In life, people who grow up with little prestige and privilege often become the most successful, because they've been squeezed and tested and have learned to endure. During the tests and trials, we are often pruned so that we can become more productive. We shed dead weight and pick up the wisdom, compassion, and resources that will help us succeed in the next place. For me, it was compassion and the vocabulary to articulate how it feels and what it means to trust God. Although I felt all alone in my moments of despair, God never left me. He was actually by my side the entire time making sure that I received what I needed to during that season. I bet if you take a look at some of your most difficult seasons, you'll notice what you gained, how God molded you and pruned you, and how that season prepared you to help the people who were assigned to you in your next place.

Trusting God is significant during a time of derailment. Despite what happens and the situations that may change around us, we serve an unchanging God. Our feelings and our circumstances tell us that it is hard to trust God or that we shouldn't trust God, but by proof of what He's done in the past, we must remember that as children of God we can always trust the Father who created us. We must trust Him even when it is uncomfortable to do so. Psalm 125:1-3 says, "Those who trust in the LORD are like Mount Zion, which cannot be shaken but endures forever. As the mountains surround Jerusalem, so the LORD surrounds his people both now and forevermore." I love this scripture since David says that when we trust in GOD, we are like unmovable mountains. It may affect the trees, it may affect the animals and everything else around it, but when a storm comes, it doesn't affect a mountain. The mountain can remain calm and durable during the storm as it knows that the winds may blow and the lightning may flash, but when the storm passes, it will remain. That's how we are when we trust in GOD. No matter what happens in our lives, we can be still and know that GOD is still in control of every situation. **Everything and everyone else around us may be affected, but when we trust God we know that after the storm passes we will remain.**

People always tell me it's always easy to say, "trust God," to someone when you're not the person going through what they are. I realize this. I know it is a challenge, but challenges are meant to pull us and push us. They make us confront our weaknesses while stepping into our strength. Friend, I'm not sure what you're going through right now. It could be financial, personal, health issues, or family matters. No matter what, I know that God has the answer and that He has met this day and even saw your end before today. He has a perfect plan for you. As you move forward into the first "reflection" moment, think about that. Meditate on the God that has created and pre-designed the path to your destiny.

Reflection: *I Trust You*

I want you to be honest here: do you trust God? When storms come, when hard times overcome you, whether those issues are concerning your finances, relationships, family, or health, are you like a sturdy mountain in the midst of trouble or more like a palm tree that moves with the wind? We're in the beginning of this process, so if you admit that you often waiver and that your faith isn't where it needs to be yet, we're going to work on it together. Now is the time to admit it, so that you can address it and adjust it. I admit that in the past I have allowed fear to overcome me during moments of uncertainty. While God doesn't give us the spirit of fear, fear is still a very real feeling. This is why we must be aware of it. The only way to truly conquer that fear is to force ourselves to put unwavering trust in God. Sometimes, this is the type of trust that makes no sense to anyone but you and God.

If you are in trouble right now, I recommend getting alone with God. If you have to cry, cry. If you must question Him, do so, but then wait for an answer. Empty your soul, quiet your spirit, and allow Him to speak to you. Journal what you feel Him saying to you. Often, that moment will serve as your moment of clarity. He will probably tell you something to the nature of, "You can trust me." God isn't like everyone else who has lied to you or let you down. He promises to never leave you; to never forsake you. It's time to get alone with God and begin to trust Him. Take a moment of quiet time alone with God now, and allow Him to talk to you. Go ahead, you can pick up right here, in Chapter Two, once you're done.

Chapter 2: *Derailment*

In a matter of forty-eight hours, I went from ministering on a platform in front of thousands to sitting in the back of a police car alone and afraid. Here's what happened. In October of 2014, my group was invited to Cape Town South Africa by Bishop Hezekiah Walker to perform for a conference. It was my first time on South African soil, and I was extremely excited to be there. My group, including my wife and band, ministered to a completely packed service, with thousands of people who were in expectation of Holy Spirit to move.

I've noticed that every time I am doing what God has called me to do, I feel right at home, no matter how far away from home I really am. When worshippers are together in God's presence, there is an indescribable, shared familiarity. That is exactly how it was on this particular night—amidst unfamiliar faces, in a place where I'd never been, I felt right at home and I poured my heart out on that stage. God truly blessed us all. The worship was so powerful and the presence of the Spirit was evident through women and men speaking in tongues, people who were completely surrendered to God— hands raised high, attendees praising, dancing, and shouting before God. Our music prompted weeping and heartfelt worship by many in attendance. We ministered with God's power for a little over an hour. The feeling was indescribable to see so many of my South African brothers and sisters singing many of my songs, like "I Trust You", "Live Through It", "I Believe", and "The Praise Break," which features Bishop Hezekiah Walker, word for word. We released "Live Through It" that year and it often shifted the atmosphere, along with another song from that album, *Let Your Power Fall,* during prophetic ministry conferences such as this one. Everyone in attendance was thirsty for the presence of God. He led us in an amazing worship service, and I was grateful to be used in such a powerful way.

During day two of this three-day trip, my music family and I spent our time sight-seeing and taking pictures. One of my favorite things to do is watch National Geographic *Wild* on television so to actually be in the country where many of these animal specials are filmed was a surreal feeling. I love seeing the exotic animals, such as lions and great white sharks, in their original habitats. While in Cape Town, I even thought about going deep sea cage diving to see the sharks up close, but my faith in the cage where I would be placed wavered so I had to rebuke that temporary urge. You're probably saying, "Why didn't you just "'trust God?'" I hear you, Saints! But let's just say that I decided to exercise wisdom this time.

After making a global impact through ministry, having fun in an element outside of our own, and connecting with the local community, we took the twenty-hour flight back home the following day. On the outside, everything *seemed* great. Yet, less than forty-eight hours later, I couldn't believe my life's 180-degree turnaround. I was sitting in a freezing cold Fort Bend County jail cell—emotions ripped apart; I was helpless.

"How did this happen? Everything was all good just two days ago," I kept thinking. Our performance on stage played in my head like a broken record. To say that I beat myself up would be an understatement. Me, myself, and I were going blow-to-blow. There were two, very different versions of myself at war at two opposing sides. There was the Past, Depressed Me on one side and the Future, Faithful Me on the other. Both were in a knock-down, drag-out, twelve-round match to the finish, and the depressed James Fortune was going for a TKO. As history would have it, the Future Me was no match for the negative emotions that overtook that moment—emotions that were deeply rooted in my past. *Dear Future Me* would have to return later. It sounds cliché, but all I could think about once I was behind bars and actually able to think clearly was, "How did I get here?"
How did I get here?

When we returned from South Africa, the following day was business as usual. I immediately got back to work. At the time, in addition to having experienced a few #1 records and international popularity, I also hosted a nationally-syndicated radio show, *The James Fortune Show*, and it was growing by the month. Segments like "Why Are You Feeling Fortunate" and "What Cha Gonna Do?" had become listener favorites all over the country. The radio show ended at 10 p.m. each night. That night, I came home, and figured that my wife was sleep since she had texted me earlier saying that she was still tired from the twenty-hour flight and she'd be calling it a night. I came home and knew that I needed to go to bed soon. The next day we would be headlining Texas Southern University's homecoming gospel celebration. I just needed a few minutes to wind down, so I went into the living room, turned on the television, and started watching sports highlights on ESPN. My kids were in the room with my wife, which wasn't unusual since they often slept in the bed with us.

As I was sitting on the couch, I noticed something odd, which at the time, seemed to confirm a suspicion I had been having for a while. It hit a nerve within me. I thought it was weird, but I decided to try and keep calm, although I could feel myself starting to boil inside. Something wasn't right. After a while, I decided to go to bed. Sure, I was still upset, but I had no plans on waking my wife up to discuss what I'd seen. I told myself that I was going to get into the bed and ask her about it the next day. *But if she wakes up, we will be talking about this tonight.* I was boiling, but I decided that the best thing I could do was to go to bed.

Like many people reading this, I later realized that perhaps I could have prayed about my response. That would have been the right thing to do… the Christian thing to do. I know, I know, but to be real with you, praying was unfortunately the last thing on my mind at that time. I was not happy—livid to be exact. I admit, I was operating in my flesh, and I was about to experience the results of that, just as the apostle Paul forewarns us. *For the flesh desires what is contrary to the Spirit, and the Spirit what is contrary to the flesh. They are in conflict with each other, so that you are not to do whatever you want* (Gal. 5:17).

When I walked in the room and started moving around, I startled my wife, who hadn't realized that I was home. We were both on the defense—her out of shock and me out of anger. I asked her a question about what I had seen and she denied what I was insinuating. I told her that she was lying. She jumped up—and both of us, emotionally charged, proceeded to ruin our marriage. Perhaps the timing of everything was off. Perhaps I was too aggressive and didn't approach her the right way; maybe her attitude and what I thought was a blatant lie pushed me over the edge. She was just waking up; I was way too tired and upset… as time ticked away inside of the Fort Bend County Jail, I ran all of these scenarios through my head, swapping out our actual reality with alternative endings that didn't result in me in an orange jumpsuit eating cold cheese sandwiches for the next forty-eight hours. Nevertheless, despite the various rumors that circulated, this is what happened. I questioned her, and we got into a heated argument. Once she denied what I was accusing her of, she said she was leaving and she was taking the kids. When she said that, my mind immediately went back to previous arguments when she had taken the kids away for days, and I had no idea where they were, and that was something that I wasn't going to let happen again.

"You can leave, but you aren't taking the kids anywhere!" I told her. As she went for our children, I grabbed her and began to pull her out of the room. She wasn't having it! Her position was *if she goes, the kids go too*. As I struggled to remove her out of the bedroom, I remember thinking, "It shouldn't be this hard to move this woman." There was something about trying to separate a mom from her kids. There was a physical strength that came over her that made her my match. She wasn't having it and plopped down on the floor and refused to move. I was finally able to get her up and put her out of the room. In the hallway outside of our bedroom, I pushed her, she slammed into the wall and hit the floor. In almost an instant, she jumped back up and we tussled back and forth, me trying to push the door closed and her trying to push the door back open. After about five seconds of that, I was able to overpower her, and I slammed the door in her face and locked it. There were two ways to get into our room, so she tried to run around to the second entrance, and I hurried to close and lock that door before she could make it to that side. I barely beat her to that door, and when I did, I slammed and locked it. She banged loudly on the door for a few minutes asking to get in the room, and I shouted back at her that I was not going to open the door. She went to the kitchen, grabbed a knife, and flew back up the stairs, attempting to pry the door open. But it wouldn't work. The kids were awake by then, and I asked them if they wanted to get in the bed with me, and they did. We all went to sleep. I figured my wife was in another room of the house once everything was silent. I also thought that our argument and this situation was over. We'd had arguments before and this one didn't seem more or less serious.

Some hours later, my oldest son woke me up and said the police were at the door and wanted to talk with his mom and me. I thought it was odd. I wondered why the police were at my house. I thought that maybe a neighbor heard us, but I quickly dismissed that thought, because we weren't loud enough to be heard outside of our home. As I was walking to the door, I wondered why my wife hadn't answered the door. The next few moments didn't make any sense to me. I literally woke up from my sleep and my wife was gone. My life changed forever, and my children witnessed it all. They hadn't seen anything but they had heard everything. The next minutes, hours, days, and even months of our lives would be our darkest to date.

I opened the door, and the cop asked, "What happened here?"

I told him, "Me and my wife got in an argument and I locked her out of our room."

"Well, did you know that your wife is at the hospital and is being examined for assault?" "No, of course not!"

"You're under arrest for Family Violence…" he told me. At the time, it didn't seem real. His mouth was moving, but I didn't hear anything else that came out of it.

"Family violence? There's no way this is serious," I thought, Yes, I pushed her and locked her out of the room. I was wrong to put my hands on her at all, but my actions at the time didn't seem like "abuse" to me. (Obviously, I had a lot to learn about abuse, which we'll discuss later.) In my natural mind, I thought, "I did not hit her. I would have never hit her, especially in front of my children. They were there the entire time. Shouldn't someone ask them if their father is an abuser?" I had seen so many stories about women being abused and I wouldn't do *that.* I had even hosted specials on my radio show and helped countless other women who had been in abusive relationships. I was hurt and confused to say the least. I couldn't imagine going to jail for abusing my wife, and so to hear those words were surreal. When I felt the handcuffs lock around my wrists, the situation elevated from surreal to absurd. My mind was racing, and the questions came a mile a minute.

"What is happening?"

"How did we get here?"

"Why did my wife go to the hospital at all, let alone say that I had assaulted her?"

"I need to clear this up right away."

We'd had similar arguments in the past. This was no different. I didn't think this situation could get any worse than it was in that moment. I was furious and in shock as I sat in the back of that cop car waiting for the officers to finish talking about the "case," and running my name through their system. It seemed like forever. One-by-one, my babies proceeded out of the house, like a short funeral procession, and in a way, it was… this night marked the death of our marriage and our family would never be the same.

Many people don't realize this, but once I was released on bail for the next few months, my wife and I actually went to counseling and tried to save our marriage. As you'll see in a little while we weren't legally supposed to be around each other but we did it anyway. We even traveled to get away and even ministered together for a few more shows. We spent that Thanksgiving and Christmas together, and actually started reconciling. Believe it or not, things were going pretty well considering the circumstances. We both wanted our marriage and our family back together.

I even remember one day she sent me a text that said, "New Love." I asked her why she went to the hospital. She told me that her body felt really sore from the fall, and she just wanted to make sure she was okay. She said that she didn't think her going to the hospital was that serious and she hadn't planned on reporting me or that incident, but the hospital workers were grilling her and didn't believe that she had just fallen on her own. One thing led to the next, and she ended up telling a nurse or two what went on between us and the police were called. This is normal procedure. Many times, nurses in hospitals are the first form of help that abuse victims are able to connect with. There are so many cases when women who are abused minimize their injuries and the seriousness of their situations. As I came to terms with what happened between us and learned more about the epidemic of domestic violence, I knew that everything that happened in the hospital was what should have occurred. Although I didn't realize I was abusing my wife, that's exactly what I had done. She left the hospital a few hours later. They examined her and then released her once they found that there were no serious injuries.

As she sat in a hospital, I was booked, processed, and put in an open area inside of the jail with other inmates. A lot of the jailers were familiar with me, so I was put in protective custody and given my own cell. I guess the authorities feared someone could have tried to cause me harm. I was finally settled (if that's even possible) around four in the morning. The night was a whirlwind. It was a really messy and unpredictable ending to a chapter that started out with me and my wife performing alongside of each other in South Africa. I could not have imagined that such a blessed experience could end this way. If someone would have told me that I'd be accused of abusing my wife, I probably would have bet the world otherwise. Nothing about this situation belonged to me. It was hard to accept and even harder to live through.

The next day, I was released. I knew that life wasn't "business as usual," but I attempted to function that way. I honestly just wanted my life to be normal again. I wanted to forget the day before, the argument, police, and image of my children walking out of the house. I tried to forget my night in jail, the new charges on my record. I wanted to forget all of it. I was disgusted by my truth and in denial of its consequences.

My wife took my son to his little league football homecoming game and had to walk him across the field alone, because I couldn't go. One of the conditions of my bail, according to the judge, was that I couldn't have contact with my wife and children. Those conditions were devastating to me. As I stood before the judge and he said I couldn't see, talk, or have any type of communication with my wife or kids I almost collapsed in the courtroom. I looked at my lawyer and she said that there was nothing she could do. The only way I could get out of jail was by agreeing to not have any contact with my family and if I did I would be brought back to jail. Without my children in my life, without being able to touch them, hug them, experience their joys and pains, my entire world was derailed. I had been through storms before, but I always had my wife and children to distract me from whatever I was going through. Their love and support outweighed anything else I was facing. Not this time. I was released from jail and I immediately drove to the radio show to make it just in time to go live. During the entire time that the show was on air, I was praying and hoping that the media would not get ahold of this story and that my family and I would be able to work through our issues privately. The worse thing that could happen would be for the press to find out. My job as a national radio show host, and more importantly, my reputation as a minister of music, would be in jeopardy. I was hopeful that no one would find out and the incidents of the day before would remain a private matter. However, not even an hour after I made it to the radio station, I began to see social media reports that I had been arrested for family violence. One news report after another surfaced and my management team began to receive excessive phone calls and requests for statements and interviews.

Many lies circulated through the media about broken bones and internal and external injuries. My lawyer and wife tried to stop these lies by agreeing to allow the news media to see her complete medical report but they didn't want to see it. The sensationalism of the story was way better for ratings. In a matter of hours, I became the topic of discussion in the gospel and mainstream music and church communities. My social media accounts were going crazy with everything from name calling to death threats and comments damning me to eternal hell. It was impossible to forget what happened, and as I was on air, the situation escalated even more in the media.

Behind-the-scenes, however, my wife and I were actually trying to work the situation out. Even though she didn't have to, she defended me and tried to clear my name in the media and tell the truth about what really happened. People were saying all types of things, and most of them were lies. Although she attempted to support me and fix the situation, it was too late. Once the story hit the news, there was no stopping the inevitable train wreck. I was extremely upset, mainly at myself. It seemed like we were losing everything. All of my concerts were cancelled.

I was suspended from the radio show, and as a result, my hope in the situation waivered. It felt like the bottom was falling out of my life's foundation—this public nightmare ripped the core of me away. One of the hardest parts of it all was the effect this had on my children. Adults confronted them and they eventually were kicked out of their Christian private school. If you are a parent, you are well aware of how it feels to see your children hurt without the power to help them. What made it worse was the guilt that I felt having caused them pain. Every parent desires for their children to live in a happy home, get a good education, and experience peace. Now this was all in jeopardy. As if this nightmare couldn't get any more terrifying, my relationships with them were in peril, since I was ordered to stay away from them. Yes, sure, we snuck around and had private visits but that wasn't enough. No matter how bad I wanted to fix the situation for my children, and for us, there was really nothing that I could do besides let it play out and pray. I was in constant agony. My heart was broken. Our lives changed so quickly. I missed my family and I lived in a constant state of anger and regret.

As the media continued to fuel the fire, my wife and I were trying to work out our marriage, but it was very hard. Even though I was wrong, I was upset as a result of everything that had transpired, including the public humiliation, that was now not just hurting us, but altering my kids' lives as well. It was like a domino effect—or more like a wildfire that couldn't be extinguished. This, of course, made reconciliation between my wife and me very hard. We also couldn't openly communicate with each other, unless we snuck around. I didn't know how situations like this worked—if the cops were following us around or if I would be arrested again by being near her. It took a toll, and after a while, we stopped speaking all together. Prior to that, however, she had tried to lie for me and told my attorney, the police, and court system that I didn't touch her at all; but her story didn't matter. Not until later during my time in domestic violence counseling did I understand that the police and legal system viewed my wife as a victim—and no matter if this ordeal and arrest had been over-exaggerated, it was not uncommon for victims of abuse to recant on their stories and defend the abuser later down the line. Often, when abuse charges are filed and arrests are made, it is no longer in the "victim's" hands or control. The county or state will prosecute these cases, regardless. Now, understanding more about abuse, and the psyche of both victims and abusers, I fully understand this. At the time, I just wanted the courts to believe me and my wife, and for all of this to just go away so that we could rebuild our broken lives.

As things got worse for me legally, career-wise, and in the media, the anger and resentment set in. I no longer wanted to work out my marriage. You probably couldn't tell from the stage, but the end of us and the situation that bought it to a head had been a long time coming. We had a lot of issues. I had not yet begun family violence therapy, and I didn't know how to fully express myself or navigate the situation. I'm not trying to make excuses for my actions; there are none. Honestly, at this time, all I could feel was anger, loss, grief, and self-pity. The mountain seemed impossible to climb, and I didn't have the energy or attitude to even try anymore.

It was ultimately my fault. I threw in the towel completely and filed for a divorce. I take full responsibility now for what happened, both on October 23, 2014 and the years before that led up to that combustible night. My anger and lack of control were the causes of our downfall.

***

I minimized that incident and never could have realized the consequences would have been so steep. I was separated from my children for months. This is when my heart crumbled and broke into a million tiny pieces. Prior to that night, I was with my children every day when I wasn't working. My oldest two were really active in sports, and being there for them was the joy of my life. I worked so much, but my kids and I always had a very special relationship. I would come home from ministry engagements on the road, and they would play sleep, and then get up and jump on me. Moments like these mean the world to fathers. Experiencing their excitement to see me was the best part of my life, period. Losing their presence hurt me deeper than I could have ever imagined. The marriage and everything that my wife and I did revolved around the kids, even down to holidays like Valentine's Day. We had a family tradition; I would date my daughters and she would date my son. Every year our family took an annual Disney World vacation. I was involved in every aspect of their lives from their school plays, sports, to other extracurricular activities. We played kickball together, and we would all relax and hang out in the house around the television. We were a unit, and as tight as any family could get.

What happened that night and in the months to come changed everything. To this day, our relationships are still not the same. The aftermath of divorce produces one of those situations that I wrote about earlier—you will never get the same exact life back, but you learn to develop a new normal per se. Today, my children love spending time with both their dad and their mom, and of course that happens separately now. I am thankful for the many memories that they have when we were all together. Divorce has hurt my family extensively, and some of us are still very upset. I was extremely mad, hurt, and depressed for quite some time; in fact, I was only able to overcome those emotions through therapy and counseling. My kids were really torn and confused by the divorce. I pray that one day their mom and I will be able to have a healthy co-parenting relationship. As of right now, I am and have been on probation from what transpired and the attorneys feel like we don't need to communicate. I speak directly with my children, who of course all have cell phones now.

How did this happen?

I'm not sure if this is true for you, but I rarely fully gain full revelation from an event or moment until much later—sometimes it takes months or years to grasp the spiritual lessons that will help me grow. As I look back on that year, I can see the words that Jesus spoke in John 10:10 vividly. He warned, *"The thief's purpose is to steal and kill and destroy. My purpose is to give them a rich and satisfying life"* (NLT). No matter how many times we hear that verse, during the heat of a moment, our challenge is to remember that "the thief" is often behind those vicious arguments, fallouts, and relationship rifts.

While in South Africa, my wife, band, and I enjoyed a rich and satisfying experience, but as soon as we let our guards down—immediately after that moment with and for God, the thief attempted to destroy our family unit. In order to do this, he used me. Do you think it was a coincidence that Satan sought to find an open door with me? He goes for the public ambassadors for Christ—the ones who are doing the most. His logic: if he can take down the head, everyone and thing under it will fall. This was his tactic when he tempted Jesus in the wilderness, and it's one that he still uses today. The point I want to stress is that whenever we are used by God in a mighty way, the enemy looks for a way to rip it all apart, and he doesn't travel too far to find that way. He pits friends against friends, ministry partners against each other, and entices husbands and wives to fall out of agreement. *I'll show him. I'll destroy them and take God's glory*—is what Satan was saying as my group and I performed for the Lord in Cape Town. Thousands of people were ministered to, their hearts healed and recovered from the grips of the devil's bondage. They experienced breakthroughs. This moment did not fare well in hell. Anyone who disrupts the kingdom of darkness as they work for the Kingdom of God has a target on his back—and Satan was determined to hit a bulls-eye with James Fortune & FIYA, with an emphasis on my wife and me.

Now, don't get me wrong. I do not blame what I have shared with you on the devil; I no longer live in the neighborhood of excuses. The devil doesn't have power over me, God has given me power and authority over him. Dr. Jim Harris, Christian executive coach and author wrote the following in a *Charisma Magazine* article, "The defeated enemy can never stop your work for the Lord—he can only delay it." God calls every believer to mature spiritually, especially as it pertains to resisting the enemy. He instructs us to put on our full armor each day to be equipped for these battles with Satan. When we don't, it's easy to fall prey. I had to fully grasp this in order to discover the answer to the question, *How did this happen?* The Apostle Paul uses the metaphor of a Roman soldier to equip us for spiritual battles. If you haven't seen a picture of one of these soldiers, I encourage you to look it up. They were tough! Every piece of a soldier's uniform was designed to serve as defense against attacks from the enemy. The full armor protected him from head to feet— this is why Paul compared our preparation to that of a soldier's of his time. We weren't designed to be left exposed. God wants us equipped. Ephesians 6:13-17 reads,

Therefore put on the full armor of God, so that when the day of evil comes, you may be able to stand your ground, and after you have done everything, to stand. Stand firm then, with the belt of truth buckled around your waist, with the breastplate of righteousness in place, and with your feet fitted with the readiness that comes from the gospel of peace. In addition to all this, take up the shield of faith, with which you can extinguish all the flaming arrows of the evil one. Take the helmet of salvation and the sword of the Spirit, which is the word of God.

When God uses you for a <u>mountaintop moment</u> for His kingdom, beware. The enemy will come in and attempt to steal-kill-and-destroy. This is the nature of Satan, and as believers, we must be fully armored. We must make sure there are no open doors for the enemy to enter. What were my open doors? My emotions toward my wife, my tendency to verbally abuse and exert power and control in our relationship, and untreated anger and pain were entryways that I left ajar. These open doors caused a major derailment for my family.

A <u>mountaintop moment </u>is one like I experienced in South Africa, or more notable moments like we read about in the Bible. For instance, Moses and the Israelites experienced one mountaintop moment after another when Moses convinced the Egyptian Pharaoh to let the Israelites leave Egypt (of course due to God's great plagues). I'm sure this was the highest moment of most—if not all—of their lives. God then parted the Red Sea, provided daily manna, and allowed them to conquer their enemies. These were mountaintop experiences. One literal mountaintop moment is the account on Mount Carmel that we read about in 1 Kings 18. The Lord instructed the Prophet Elijah to confront King Ahab and challenge the false prophets of Baal. Elijah stepped to King Ahab and told him to bring all of his false prophets to Mount Carmel. Verse 21-26 (NIV) reads:

Elijah went before the people and said, "How long will you waver between two opinions? If the Lord is God, follow him; but if Baal is God, follow him."

But the people said nothing.

Then Elijah said to them, "I am the only one of the Lord's prophets left, but Baal has four hundred and fifty prophets. Get two bulls for us. Let Baal's prophets choose one for themselves, and let them cut it into pieces and put it on the wood but not set fire to it. I will prepare the other bull and put it on the wood but not set fire to it. Then you call on the name of your god, and I will call on the name of the Lord. The god who answers by fire—he is God."

Then all the people said, "What you say is good."

Elijah said to the prophets of Baal, "Choose one of the bulls and prepare it first, since there are so many of you. Call on the name of your god, but do not light the fire." So they took the bull given them and prepared it.

Then they called on the name of Baal from morning till noon. "Baal, answer us!" they shouted. But there was no response; no one answered. And they danced around the altar they had made.

After taunting these false prophets for hours, Elijah told the people to come close as he prepared an alter with wood and stone and poured water onto it for the Lord. Then he prayed to God, and God lit a fire under it. Afterwards, Elijah had the false prophets of Baal seized and he killed them. This was a great mountaintop moment.

Right after that, however, the enemy mobilized one of his strongest operatives, Queen Jezebel, who sent word to Elijah that she would kill him just like he did her prophets within a day's time. The Bible says that Elijah was scared. He left his servant in Beersheba (the prophet isolated himself), then ran for his life, hid in a cave, and prayed for God to let him die. As I reflected on my time in jail, immediately after my mountaintop experience in Africa, I was reminded of Elijah. I'm pretty sure Elijah asked himself, "How did this happen?" as he sat there alone, depressed, and begging to die. He had the same questions and conversations with God as I did during various times in my life—*I'm doing what you called me to do God... I am serving your people, spreading your name, giving you glory and honor, people are even getting saved as a result of the ministry you've given me... so, how could you allow the enemy to attack me like this?*

Read Elijah's story once again. I'm not sure about how it affected you, but when I read that and imagine the prophet in that moment, I can definitely relate. I've questioned God in the same way as I wrestled with derailment. If you are in a place where you too are wondering, "How did this happen?" perhaps my process of self-realization will help you. For me, I had to realize that my derailment was my fault. It's that simple. For you it may be different, because derailments aren't always the result of personal fault. My pastor used to always say that "Everything that happens to you is about you, it's not about the other person. God is trying to do something in you." By putting the attention on self-responsibility, we push through the victim mindset and we are able to stop blaming others. I had to get to the point of admitting my faults (which I will share more about later) before I could gain the full revelation of how I was derailed. As a result of this process, I learned that I had left some doors open. There were open doors and unresolved issues that provided an entryway to this major life derailment. One of my main open doors was my emotions and overlooking damage in the foundation of my relationship. Anything left untreated gets worse. We cannot run from issues or hide from trouble as if our hiding will make them go away.

For Elijah, his own success and victory made Jezebel attack him. Success often breeds attacks. When God's hand is on our lives, the enemy gets furious. This is true for every child of God. We are targeted because God favors us and this favor makes us victorious. In Chapter 19, when Ahab told Jezebel about Elijah's victory and that he executed the false prophets, Jezebel sent a messenger to Elijah, saying, "So let the gods do to me, and more also if I do not make your life as the life of one of them tomorrow about this time" (Verse 2). Elijah grew fearful of Jezebel and her threats, and in the very next verse, he ran for his life. Elijah had a choice to make in that moment. He could have trusted that just as God proved Himself hours before and allowed Elijah to be victorious, God would also allow Elijah to defeat Queen Jezebel. Instead, Elijah's response was to run in fear of death at the hands of the queen.

After a successful mountaintop moment, Elijah allowed fear to force him to run for his life, which temporarily diverted his course and purpose, which was to turn the people of Israel away from sin and back to God.

Elijah's fear forced him into a cave where he spent the night. The Lord came to Elijah in his cave and asked him, "What are you doing here…?" Elijah's fear still gripped him to the point where he thought that he was the only prophet still fighting for the Lord in Israel. God opened his eyes, gave him direction, told him to anoint new kings in Israel and Syria, and to also anoint Elisha as the new prophet to take the place of Elijah. I often wonder if Elijah's fear caused his mission for God to be aborted. God had a plan for Elijah and his lack of trust caused the prophet to be derailed.

We can learn so much as we consider the causes of our own derailments. Most importantly, trust in God can help prevent us from going off track and trust in God will get us back on. We cannot trust God while also fearing man. We cannot trust God while also taking matters in our own hands (like I did by allowing my emotions to overtake me). Derailments are often preventable.

Reflection: *Derailment*

Before you go onto the next chapter, consider everything you've read, learned, and digested in this one. I challenge you to consider the derailment you have experienced by writing out your reflections below.

How did it happen?

_____

_____

_____

_____

Did the enemy have an open door?

_____

_____

_____

_____

Were there untreated past issues that you failed to address?

_____

_____

_____

_____

_____

If yes, what were they?

_____

_____

_____

_____

_____

Did you have a negative collision with someone or something?

_____

_____

_____

_____

_____

Were you moving too fast without carefully considering your actions?

_____

_____

_____

_____

_____

Did you fall into fear and out of trust of God?

_____

_____

_____

_____

How will you develop a deeper trust in God?

_____

_____

_____

_____

Chapter 3: *Broken Rails*

There were people who attended high school with me who were derailed by cycles of drug abuse, sex, prostitution, promiscuity, and alcoholism. Some of these individuals seem to repeat the same cycles in their lives over and over. The horrible consequence of bad cycles is that if we do not stop them, they will breed more bad cycles—more derailments. Drug abuse will often open the door to incarceration and violence. Promiscuity can lead to birthing children who never know their fathers. Prostitution opens the door to shame, regret, and low self-esteem. Bad cycles produce more bad cycles—it's never a one stop derailment. Jonathan McReynolds explains this concept in his song "Cycles." In it he explains how the devil wants to make sequel cycles and he learns from our mistakes even when we don't.

Often issues like pride, refusal to take responsibility, lack of outside help, bitterness, and a failure to forgive enable destiny derailments to permanently alter the course of people's lives. These traits cause repeat cycles, and when this happens, instead of experiencing a derailment, people experience a complete standstill where their lives stop moving forward, or worse, travel backwards. Without intervention, destiny derailments that could have been fixed with care and attention become permanent stops and breaks in life.

Once I solidified the title of this book, oddly, I began to notice an influx of train crashes and derailments. News outlets broadcasted details of train derailments in some part of the world almost weekly. On February 12, 2018, the Independent, a UK publication headline read AUSTRIA TRAIN

CRASH: AT LEAST ONE DEAD AND MORE THAN 22 PEOPLE INJURED IN NIKLASDOR RAIL COLLISION **Several carriages derailed after intercity train collides with local service near central town of Niklasdorf.**[1] The cause of this derailment was a collision—one train hit another. A February 5, 2018, a CNN headline read: **2 killed, 116 hurt when Amtrak train crashes into stationary freight train.**

In the previous chapter, I posed the question, How did this happen? Wisdom tells us to examine the causes and reasons for accidents and tragedies after-the-fact, to learn the contributing factors and how to prevent them from happening again. History proves that derailments are the top causes of train crashes, according the Federal Railroad Administration. A derailment means that a train veers of its tracks. While the majority of the train accidents we hear about were caused by derailments, there are a number of other causes, including speed, mechanical malfunctions, and foreign objects that find their way on the tracks. I had no clue that derailments would be the top cause of train accidents. It makes total sense, however. Derailments have been a part of life since Adam and Eve were in Eden. Consider the various situations that come against your destiny each year. A wrong move, bad relationship, or negative reaction can change the entire course of your life forever.

Once I dug a little bit deeper, I learned that for the purpose of this book there is also a serious need to examine the cause of derailments.[2] I learned that broken rails is the top contributing factor for train derailments. It probably wouldn't be too far off base then if we were to say that something broken in a person's structure is a key cause for a destiny derailment. When rails break, trains derail, and when our foundational structures break, including relationships, family, or career, we experience destiny derailments. Passengers, train conductors, and the general public put their trust in railways to be dependable thoroughfares to enable a train to travel from one place to the next. In the same manner, we naturally consider relationships, family, and careers to provide trustworthy pathways to help us to move from one stop to the next in our life journeys. Brokenness significantly alters those plans.

Live Through It

Following major catastrophes, public embarrassment, and loss of life associated with train derailments, the companies must figure out how to live through the mess that has been created, while also easing public anxiety. For you and me, things are no different. In addition to navigating the sudden shock and disappointment from being away from my family, I experienced media scrutiny and hate like I had never experienced before. At first I started to defend myself. The anger and bitterness from the divorce and separation from my children overtook me. I had never realized it before, but I was broken, my relationship was broken, and I had deeply embedded issues of power, control, and a lack of positive communication in my relationship that went unaddressed, just like those broken rails.

I was separated from my family, and many people who I thought were my friends turned their backs on me. I tried to go to church, but the looks and stares from people in the pulpit and the pews were too much. One pastor in Houston sent me a message stating that "we don't allow criminals in our church." The church was all I had known since I was five-years-old playing the drums at my dad's house of worship. If I wasn't welcomed at church where could I go? I really fell into a deep, dark hole. My mental state started to change. I literally felt like I was losing my mind. I started forgetting things, sleeping in late, losing track of days, letting important things slip… my mind was literally going. I was falling into a depression that was foreign to me. I was isolated. I was losing it. Like Job, I even cursed the day I was born, and like Elijah, I asked God to let me die. I had such a strong dislike for the person that I saw in the mirror, and I couldn't blame anyone but myself. I didn't feel like I deserved to be on earth anymore. I didn't love myself.

The emotional and mental place where I found myself was a space that the devil desires every believer to be. Satan has nearly won the battle for our healthy lives when the derailments cause a lack of self-love, lack of desire to live, lack of self-worth, and an inability to trust God. When we lose hope, it's easy to lose everything else, including life. Hope deferred makes the heart sick (Prov. 13:12). If you are in place where you have lost hope, keep reading, because the remainder of this chapter is going to bless you. I pray that your hope is revived as you see how God can work a miracle in the direst and desolate situations. It's time that you

> # Refocus on the God who specializes in reviving the hopeless and resurrecting the dead.

As long as there is still breath in your body, you are still more than a conqueror.

During this time, I had been taking Xanax, an antidepressant, and one night, I looked at the bottle and thought, "Swallowing this entire bottle is a peaceful and easy way to end it all." As I put all the pills in my mouth, and even swallowed a few, I suddenly coughed, and some of the pills flew out of my mouth and across the bed. I grabbed them off of the comforter and started putting them back in my mouth. Then God showed me the faces of my kids. I froze immediately. Being away from them for months had been the most difficult and painful experience I had ever been through in life. As I sat there with a Xanax bottle in my hand, God said to me, "You've been telling everyone else to, 'Live Through It,' and now it's time for you to do what you've been encouraging others to do. You have to live through this." I spit the pills out in my toilet, picked up my phone, and found my song. I sat and wept for hours as "Live Through It" played over and over. The beginning of the healing process had finally begun.

That night, through all of the tears, I believe that the thick layers of denial and pride rolled away and I saw the truth for what it really was. Brokenness. After making a lot of excuses and blaming other people, I had to realize that ultimately I was responsible. Just as I was responsible for this derailment, I would have to be responsible for getting my life back on track.

God had a plan for me, and it was up to me to live through it long enough to discover what His plan was.

I enrolled in counseling first and began a life-changing journey. Many men (and women) have a negative view of seeking counseling for mental health. Men often suppress their emotions. We hide the sadness and pain and express these feelings in the form of anger and aggression. Some turn to drugs and alcohol. Psychology Today referred to men's mental health (and our lack of treatment) as a "silent crisis." Seventy-five percent of suicide victims are men. "Many men report negative experience in family courts, with data suggesting that only about one in six men have custody of their children, often with minimal visitation rights. This separation and loss can be soul-destroying for the men concerned, again leaving them isolated and alienated from mainstream society. As such, substance abuse may be a maladaptive response to a malevolent situation."[3] I was a common statistic and high suicide risk at this time and didn't even know it. I encourage all men who have dealt with or are dealing with similar situations to seek help in the form of licensed, experienced mental health professionals.

Men have a tendency to allow pride to keep us from seeking the help we need for sensitive issues such as domestic violence, divorce, custody battles, and social isolation. This was me at first, but a real turning point took place when I sought real help and took accountability for my actions. Ultimately, I was the issue. That doesn't mean that other people didn't influence the circumstances or that I hadn't been hurt. It meant that I was ready to take accountability and realize that I had to take control of my destiny if I ever wanted to get back on course and heal. I desperately wanted to become a better man, a better father, and a better child of God. Focusing on what others had done didn't get me anywhere and wouldn't get me anywhere. Playing the victim wasn't helping me move out of that dark hole and bottomless pit that had become my home. Focusing on other people kept me stuck; when I redirected my energy to accountability and healing, I began to move forward—the train was in motion again.

When I took responsibility and accountability things started to change for me. Gaining an awareness of my past actions, through family violence counseling with a group of ten other men, was like having scales removed from my eyes and seeing my former marriage for what it was. I felt like God was releasing me.

In therapy, I would learn that a lack of self-love, or self-love that was defined by public affirmation, was actually another broken area in my soul foundation. Others' opinions of us should not validate or define the opinion we have of ourselves. This is a common problem that people who have a large following yet low self-esteem deal with. It's easy to base your self-worth on popularity or material possessions, and even easier to hide how broken and hurt we are inside. I am a proponent of therapy and counseling, because life happens every day and too often we don't talk about the issues we face on a day-to-day basis. Before we know it, a once healthy and productive person can be broken and bitter as their self-worth and esteem are chipped away by the abuses of life on a daily basis. Therapy helps us to confront these truths and release our pains.

When I started counseling, I thought abuse was strictly about keeping your cool and not using your hands. However, in counseling, I learned that there are sixteen different forms of abuse. Intimidation, coercion and threats, economic abuse (controlling a spouse's finances), emotional abuse (put downs, making her feel bad about herself, name calling, humiliating her), isolation, using children to make her feel bad... all of these behaviors are also forms of abuse. Most people are just like me and we think of abuse as physical violence and sexual assault, but it goes so much deeper than that. In our world today, the reality is that abuse can range from physical assault to emotional, verbal, cyber, financial, spiritual, and so on. One guy who was in therapy with me was arrested for sending abusive text messages. At the time, he didn't realize that he was breaking the law and abusing his spouse when their heated arguments led to him sending those words to her phone. This group counseling was a much-needed intervention that God used to mature me, wake me up to the truth about myself, and make me more aware of the toxicity that I had allowed in my past relationships. Although my marriage was over, I truly regretted how we wrote our love story and my deepest desire was to never repeat those same mistakes again.

Learning about the different types of domestic violence affected me. I recognized how many times that I was abusive and didn't realize it. Studying the different forms of abuse was one of the main steps in my journey that helped me become accountable. I learned that domestic violence is often about power and control—exerting yourself to get your way, and that it doesn't always have to be about anger. I realized how long we as men had been gender trained to be "the man of the house," that men are supposed to "be strong and not let our women be disrespectful," that we're supposed to "keep our houses in order"—these attitudes are even promoted in church with misinterpretations of scriptures that say women should be submissive. I didn't understand what that meant at first, and most men take those scriptures to mean that women are supposed to be obedient and docile. In actuality, it has nothing to do with obedience. Many quote Ephesians 5:22-31, which talks about wives submitting to husbands and husbands loving wives. Yet we often skip Verse 21 which reads, "Submit yourselves to one another because of your reverence for Christ." A marriage is about mutual submission and respect for one another to create a harmonious relationship and live as one. In my past quest for power and control over my household, I had abandoned the biblical mandate to submit and genuinely love my wife.

When we are broken, change begins within. As I applied this new knowledge to my life and went deeper in the Word for greater revelation from God, I started to transform. Counseling challenged my view on relationships, my view of self, and required me to make an internal change that eventually extended outward. Although, the physical circumstances of my family hadn't changed just yet and neither did the public's perception of me, there was an inward change that I knew was affecting me beyond what anyone could see. This was root work. I had finally allowed God to dig down deep below my surface to the root of all the brokenness, which was planted in my foundation. This root work was extremely necessary. I was finally at a place where I could recognize and admit my personal faults. Amidst the growth that I had experienced in the gospel industry, the beautiful children that I had raised, and the fame and success that I had come to know, I had ignored the weeds. Through therapy, we uprooted them. I replaced those weeds with seeds of love, patience, and self-control. I was making progress and it was one of the best feelings that I have experienced to date. To finally be free from anger, control, and toxic behavior—to finally be aware of what had held me back, to finally be free to admit my faults (and grow from them) in a safe environment is exhilarating. As painful as the process is, it is absolutely necessary. I imagine the same is true in the case of train derailments.

As much as Amtrak dreads the aftermath of serious, deadly derailments, some solace comes when an outside agency such as the NTSB uncovers a deadly issue that can prevent future derailments and save lives. If you know that you have "broken rails" that continue to derail your destiny, I urge you to commit to fixing them. Don't put the pressure on yourself to do it alone either. Remember, you were not created to live life in isolation and God certainly doesn't expect you to grow and rebuild your life alone. He wants to partner with you and send you people and resources to speed up the process. The broken rails were temporary. It's time to reconstruct your foundation.

After spending time in counseling and learning about domestic violence and abuse, I started helping other people heal and return to their destiny paths. I learned that one broken season of our lives does not have to determine the rest of our lives. Our great conductor, God, can fix us, even after derailments.

Reflection: *Broken Rails*

Train accidents are frequently the culmination of a sequence of events, and a variety of conditions or circumstances that may have contributed to its occurrence.

– Federal Railroad Administration Office of Safety Analysis

There may be numerous factors and conditions that caused your derailment, but you are still here and God still has a purpose for your life. He still has a plan for your future, and His promises still apply to you. I realized that I had *broken rails*. Are you like me in the sense that there have been some broken areas in your past? Taking responsibility and accountability are the first steps to healing from those broken areas. Counseling helped me get to that point. What are the broken areas that you need to address? What will be your next plan of action to begin your healing process?

Write the broken areas that you need to address:

_____

_____

_____

_____

_____

_____

Write five steps to your healing process:

_____

_____

_____

_____

_____

Chapter 4: *Identity Theft*

I'm sure you've heard of the term "identity theft." This usually refers to the fraudulent acquisition and use of a person's identity for financial gain. The victim of identity theft typically spends months or years clearing their names and financial records, and this person is forever impacted, not only financially but also emotionally. Through my experience, I've learned that identity theft is not always financial in nature. Many people experience identity theft as a result of life's derailments. The unfortunate result of identity theft is that without realizing it, people tend to consent to the new identities applied to them. Let me put this into perspective a bit.

Until 2014, throughout my time in ministry, I had always been known as "The Encourager" because of my most popular songs. I was known as the artist who created music that was able to help pull people through some of the most painful seasons of their lives. I've been able to minister through song because, God ministers to me through the same lyrics I write. I know what it feels like to lose everything and to fight for faith even when it doesn't make sense. I've realized that my transparency is what draws people close, especially in an age when we often feel like we can't be ourselves—even within the church. I can't even begin to tell you the countless emails, Facebook messages, and Instagram posts from people who have told me that one or more of my songs had literally saved their lives. I was always extremely humbled and grateful that God was using me to minister to the hurt, broken, and lost. On the day of my life derailment in 2014, I felt nothing like an encourager. I went from encouragement to complete embarrassment. From James Fortune *The Minister* to James Fortune *The Hypocrite* who was never called by God. My identity had been stolen.

Many times when we go through a derailment or setback in our lives, we can easily become so consumed by guilt, shame, anger, and other people's opinions of us that our true identities in Christ can become lost in an ocean of regret and resentment. Often, the enemy steals our identities so subtly that we don't even realize that it is happening. Negative words about us will seem to confirm negative thoughts that we were already thinking about ourselves. Those words become water to the seeds of self-doubt that were planted from derailment. Then the seeds begin to grow because of criticism, shame, and more negative words that give them energy. Before long, the confidence and identity in Christ that we once had has been replaced by a false identity that was constructed by the enemy with the purpose of oppressing us and stopping the plans God has in our lives. The thoughts and reruns of our unfortunate situations can cause us to forget that we are not the mistakes we have made; we are not what we have been through, and we are not who people may say we are.

Identity theft will cause you to forget that God never intended for the derailment that you experienced to become your final destination. In fact, as believers and members of the body of Christ, God has actually promised us just the opposite. We are under a spiritual contract with the Lord—a new covenant of grace—that He will turn our derailments around and make them work for our good, no matter what they are. This is what Romans 8:28 means for us, *"And we know that all things work together for good to them that love God, to them who are the called according to his purpose."* The scripture begins, "And we know…" The Apostle Paul wanted all believers who would ever read that sentence from his letter to the church to KNOW that ALL THINGS would WORK TOGETHER for our good. I believe that God put a burden on me to write this book and to share this concept of identity theft with you to make you aware of what has been happening in your life concerning the mistakes that you've made or the unfortunate situations that you have experienced. The enemy wants you to live defeated. He wants you to forget that you have the victory over all things.

In the gospel of Luke, Jesus selected seventy-two disciples to go out to do ministry work, which included healing the sick and performing exorcists on demon-possessed people. When they returned to give Him a report of how their mission went, they were extremely excited to share, "Lord, even the demons obey us when we use your name!" (Luke 10:17). I imagine that Jesus smiled as he witnessed His disciples awaken to their identity in HIM. He confirmed them even more and increased their confidence with His reply, "I saw Satan falling from heaven as a flash of lightning! And I have given you authority over all the power of the enemy, and you can walk among snakes and scorpions and crush them. Nothing will injure you" (Luke 10:18-19). That is so powerful. Jesus wants you to realize that you have the power over the lies, attacks, and accusations of the enemy.

When I speak of "identity theft" in this chapter, I am referring to when your issue or condition has stolen your identity. This identity theft is an illegal act of the enemy, and God does not intend for him to get away with this thievery—but unless we know that this identity theft has occurred and that it is against the laws of our divine victory in Christ, Satan will get away with his crime. Even now as I write this, I believe **the Lord is saying that He wants US to arrest Satan for his criminal activity**. So many Christians live passively, without ever activating the power that Christ has given them to walk on snakes and crush them. It's time to stop waiting for "the Lord to move," when He has given us the authority to move according to the power of His name and the strength of His Spirit. It's very dangerous to allow the enemy to get away with the crime of identity theft, because when this happens, in your mind, and in the minds of others, you are no longer known by your name, but like the man in Luke chapter six, whose name was never mentioned, you are known by your issue. God wants you to know that your issue does not—nor did it ever—define you. When you were reborn by the Spirit into the family of the Most High God, He gave you a ton of new names and a wonderful new identity, which is RIGHTEOUS. This is not due to anything that you did, but only due to Jesus. Because of Jesus, no matter what you do or experience, God still considers you righteous since when He looks at you, He sees Jesus, instead of you. This is the reason why a derailment is not a destination and why it is only a *Destiny Derailed.* Jesus faced a derailment. On that Friday on the cross, He looked defeated to everyone. He had been walking around for three years, telling people that He was the Son of God and the King of the Jews, yet He was hanging on a cross after being beat to near death. He was helpless and it looked like His identity was anything but the Messiah, the Son of God. Yet, we know the final report on Sunday morning. We know that the derailment that occurred on Friday, the cross nor the grave, were the final destinations. Jesus not only resurrected from the grave, but He became "the Resurrection." He released His Spirit to us, and gave us His power, which means just as He is, we are in this world. We too will resurrect and so will the dead, derailed situations in our lives.

The man with the withered hand in Luke chapter six is only known by that issue, his withered hand. We don't know his name, but we do know his condition. His issue had stolen his identity. I'm sure he was embarrassed and I'm sure he dealt with a lot of pain and despair because of his hand. He probably tried to hide it when he went out in public. Imagine how hard it must have been to communicate with people and be confident in his conversations knowing that he had a deformity that overshadowed his life. People didn't care about his birth name, they only called him by his condition. They had no idea that in just a few moments because of this man's encounter with Jesus, his current condition would not be his final conclusion. He encountered Jesus withered, but he would leave Him whole. Now I'll talk about this a little later when I deal with overcoming rejection, but in the very next verse after this man's hand was restored, the Bible says that the Pharisees were furious and angry at this man's restoration. When GOD restores you and you rebuild what was broken, don't expect everyone to celebrate with you. Some people will be furious that you are no longer that person who is less than they considered you to be. Your wholeness is going to remind some people of their brokenness. That's not your problem. Don't let their disposition top your celebration. Now let's make sure you understand the importance of not losing your identity after a setback...

During this time after my derailment, God brought me to the Parable of the Lost Son in Luke 15:11-32. One day, the youngest son in this story asked his father to give him his inheritance, and the father obliged. A few days later, the son gathered all of his possessions, went to a far country and wasted his inheritance on lavish living. Basically he was living it up. If he were in today's times, we could suspect that this dude would have been out at the strip clubs or partying with his boys in nightclubs, poppin' bottles and entertaining women. He might have even been smoking weed, drinking, and having sex with the women who only wanted him for his money. Basically, he got paid on a Friday and partied for a few weeks without considering what would happen when all the money was gone. Can you relate or have you ever heard about anyone doing this before?

Okay, so after he had spent all of his money, a severe famine hit the land and the son was no longer able to provide for himself. He began working in a field feeding pigs, and he was still starving and in dire need of help. As Jesus explained, this prodigal son was so desperate that he gladly would have filled his stomach with the same food that the pigs ate, yet no one gave him anything. The parable continues, "But when he came to himself, he said, 'How many of my father's hired servants have bread enough and to spare, and I perish with hunger! I will arise and go to my father, and will say to him, 'Father, I have sinned against heaven and before you, 'and I am no longer worthy to be called your son. Make me like one of your hired servants" (Verses 17-19). When he went back to his father to repent, the father didn't make the boy like one of his servants. The father didn't even require him to beg. The boy's simple act of turning back from his sinful ways (repentance) was enough for the father to completely restore him. In an act of compassion, the father in this story ran towards his son and kissed him. This gracious and loving father then instructed his servants to prepare a great celebration in honor of his son's return. They put the best robe on him, gave him a ring, sandals, and killed a fatted cow for them to eat. Basically, they had a big party! Imagine him coming home to a huge celebration with all of his friends, being gifted with the best fashions, eating his favorite food, dancing to the best live music, and having fun with everyone in the town who were all there just to honor him. This definitely caught him by surprise. Remember, this prodigal son was willing to take on the identity of a servant, someone outside of his   father's family, just to survive. Instead, the father reminded his son of his true identity. Simply because he turned away from the sinful lifestyle and the negative things that had taken him off course, the son was back like he never left!

The father made a big deal about his son's return. He didn't give him what he deserved, instead he treated him as a beloved son. Verse 24 reads, "For this my son was dead and is alive again; he was lost and is found." The son was restored to his rightful place in the family as if the derailment had never occurred. God showed this story to me and explained that He would restore me as well. Just as that father loved his son, I am His son and I am loved. What I had done did not steal my identity or God's love for me. Sometimes, the decisions we make will cause a derailment, but God doesn't give us what we deserve—He doesn't count us off as children, and He never leaves any of us behind. He only requires our repentance—meaning our 180 degree turn around in the opposite direction. He is our father, and good fathers love their children unconditionally, even when we make mistakes. Knowing this with all of your heart is significant as you mend your life back together following a derailment.

The other element that I love about this story is that the prodigal son was blessed and reminded of his true identity even in the presence of his biggest hater, which happened to be his own brother. Earlier I mentioned that not everyone will be willing to celebrate your restoration. This is very important, as oftentimes, the people who want to remind you of your derailments are those who live under the same roof. Sometimes, that person will be your husband or wife, your brother or sister, and even your mother or father. The people closest to you will always believe that they know you best, and if they believe that you are still *this* or *that*, then according to them, that is your identity. Knowing your identity in Christ is crucial, as even when your brothers or sisters reject you and fail to forgive you, God still does and

He wants you to forgive yourself as well. In this story, the father represents God. He is a good father and He always wants us to be in right standing with Him. He is always willing to forgive us, no matter how bad our mistakes were, how broken our tracks become, and how long we are derailed. **As you hear the criticism from people who are close to you, I want you to remember that the father blessed the prodigal son right in front of his own brother, despite his hater ways.**

Remembering your identity in Christ and that God has forgiven you will be key to your restoration and healing process. Romans 8:1 confirms that, *"There is therefore now no condemnation for those who are in Christ Jesus."* It's important to remember this and other verses that affirm your identity in Christ. Your identity in Christ is the real you, the you that God created you to be before you were even conceived. The world may condemn you and determine that you are not worthy of a second chance. The world may call you a liar, a thief, an abuser, worthless… but you know through the Bible that God says that you are delivered and restored. You are a child of God and that is your identity.

Destiny derailments threaten our self-esteem and self-worth, and so just as you take responsibility and accountability for your actions, get back in touch with your identity. Who does God say that you are and what did He call you to do? More than anything, hold on to the answers to those questions. I highly recommend reading passages like the blessings on obedience in Deuteronomy 28 when God tells us that He will make us the head and not the tail, above and not beneath, blessed going in the city and coming out. Read the Apostle Paul's letter to the Roman church, and 2 Corinthians 2:14, which tells us, *"Now thanks be to God who always leads us in triumph in Christ, and through us diffuses the fragrance of His knowledge in every place. For we are to God the fragrance of Christ among those who are being saved and among those who are perishing."* You are triumphant. You are the fragrance of Christ. You have His aroma; you were created in His image, and you have dominion over the world that may come against you. (Gen. 1:26)

Three of the four gospels introduce us to a "woman with the issue of blood," who had been bleeding for twelve years before she touched Jesus' garment and received instant healing. I believe that a major takeaway that God wants us to receive from this story is that the world will identify us by our issues, but God declares us healed and whole—and it doesn't take forever for us to receive our healing either. As we read in the *Parable of the Lost Son,*

> # God doesn't make us jump through hoops or prove ourselves like the world does.

All we need to do is to get into the presence of our savior and believe in faith that He controls our destiny. We never learned the bleeding woman's name; we only know her past issue. She dealt with a classic case of identity theft. Centuries later, society still does what they did to her: identify people by issues that Jesus has since healed.

Unfortunately, after we make mistakes that go public, people identify us by our issues and the worst decisions we've made in life. In order to get through this stage in my journey, I had to 1) remember who God created me to be; 2) remind myself of the many times God came through for me during hard times; and 3) recall all the various situations I made it through with Christ on my side. Once I had been empowered through counseling and personal ministry moments with God, I was empowered by the mere fact that I serve a God who cannot fail, and that same God was on my side. **Your past actions do not determine your identity and your present circumstances do not define your destiny.** Your destiny was *derailed,* not denied. Let's arrest the enemy for the assault that he has caused and the identity theft that he has committed. The only way to do that is to confront these lies boldly with the truth, which is the Word of God. Remind the enemy of your identity in Christ.

Defending Lies

As I was going through my divorce in the aftermath of the abuse charges, I still had a kingdom assignment. I was involved in the industry and was visible on social media for a while. I noticed immediately how I had been labeled as "the gospel singer who was arrested for domestic violence." That was very difficult for me. I knew that the person being described was not the man I was, even though it was something that I allowed myself to get caught up in over time. I felt like I would never be able to prove myself to these people who identified me by my past issue. Eventually, I realized that I could not change some people's perceptions of me, but God reminded me that my destiny was not going to be determined by those people's opinions.

There is a quote by Mark Twain that says, "A lie can travel halfway around the world while the truth is putting on its shoes." Prior to October 23, 2014, I had defended, deflected, minimized, and made excuses my entire life, and so automatically, I defended the rumors, tried to explain the truth, and attempted to change public opinion regarding lies. I fell into the trap of defending the lies that were being said about me. I hadn't realized that the truth didn't need an explanation, nor should I go about explaining myself to others who were not a part of the situation. Defending lies is another waste of time and energy, as often there is nothing that can be said to change the minds of people who believe the lies they are spreading. **We have God to defend us and to repair any damage that has been done by anyone spreading untruths.** We only need to cast our cares.

It got to a point when I was extremely distraught, bitter, and I desperately needed wise counsel. I couldn't understand how I could be villainized despite all the good that I had done prior to this. I talked with Bishop I.V. Hilliard, Founding Pastor of New Light Church in Houston, and he said to me, "James, don't read what they're saying about you online and in the media. If you can avoid doing that, your faith can remain intact. But if you look at that stuff, it's going to shake your faith and it's going to damage you in more ways than you can imagine." It was so true. Whenever I'd post something, I knew someone would write a negative comment. The truth and my past didn't matter. To the public, in the world, and unfortunately even in some church circles, I was labeled as "The Abuser." When Bishop Hilliard gave me that advice, I stopped looking at social media and I stayed offline for quite some time. I instructed my family and friends who were close to me not to tell me anything that people were writing or sharing online. Eventually, I was very grateful for Bishop Hilliard's wise words. If we aren't careful during vulnerable moments, outsiders can influence us and cause our faith to waiver by planting thoughts in our minds that create insecurities and keep us in a prison of past failures.

As you rebuild after a derailment, you may need to take some time out for yourself. It's a good idea to remove yourself from situations (or social media sites) that constantly remind you of missteps and mistakes from your past. It is important to stay positive, feed your mind with inspirational and empowering words, songs, and messages, and confess the Word of God over yourself. Philippians 4:8 says, "Finally, brothers and sisters, whatever is true, whatever is noble, whatever is right, whatever is pure, whatever is lovely, whatever is admirable – if anything is excellent or praiseworthy – think about such things. Your thoughts concerning your situation and yourself are so important right now. As a man thinketh in his heart, so is he. You cannot afford to suffer from identity theft during a time like this. Those who stay in a derailed state, often remain stagnant because they don't believe (or don't know) what God says about them. God hasn't changed His mind about you. Others have made the opinions of naysayers their gods and the words from these negative people become crippling. I do not want this to be you, so right here, right now, I want you to make the declaration: **GOD'S WORD ABOUT ME IS THE FINAL SAY AND WILL NOT BECOME A VICTIM OF IDENTITY THEFT.**

Write that statement here:

_____

_____

_____

_____

_____

_____

Now repeat it out loud.

I continued to seek more advice, and that journey led me to Dallas to meet with Bishop T.D. Jakes. I felt embarrassed and truly disappointed in myself that this circumstance was the impetus for our meeting. Bishop Jakes gave me a lot of good advice and he made me aware of the climate that we were living in at the time and how our culture currently viewed violence against women. He said, "One of the problems you have right now is that so many women have been abused in relationships and a lot of these women are going to see you as that same person who abused them." He was very honest. He was disappointed and he let me know it. However, he also told me that I could make it through after some time away from the spotlight, alone with GOD.

During therapy sessions in the months to follow, I would often remember Bishop Jakes' words. Then later down the line, after I started to share my story and perspective on domestic abuse, women would come to me and say, "Thank you." Their abusers never apologized and had instead always told them that it was their fault. I realized that what Bishop Jakes' told me was truer than I knew at the time. Since many of these women viewed me in the same way as their abusers, me standing up taking responsibility, helped them heal. Together, we dismantled lies that had brainwashed them and their shame was erased. My honesty helped them realize that abuse wasn't a mistake. A mistake by definition is an error in judgement or a misunderstanding. **Abuse is not a mistake; abuse is a decision**. I helped them understand that there was nothing they could have done to prevent it from happening. It was not their fault that they had been hurt. It was their abusers' fault. Through these experiences, I learned that God had the power an intention to transform my lowest moment and most embarrassing circumstances into situations that would heal His children and bring Him glory. He was able to transform my transparency into moments of healing for the women I ministered to. The restoration that took place also helped me in my recovery process and encouraged me to continue to share the truth.

Don't run from your truth, deny, or try to hide from your past. When others bring up your past, remember God's promise in Hebrews 8:12: *"I will forgive their sins and remember them no more."* If GOD says that he no longer remembers your sins once He has forgiven you, why would you allow others to constantly remind you of them?

One of the ways that helps me to grow is to figure out the lessons in the uncomfortable situations that I face. Ask yourself: why is He allowing me to experience these moments of identity theft? What could He want to communicate through me? We often get offended, hurt, or angry when people say negative things about us and refer to us by our past. If we would stop and consider how God wants to move through us, we would be better off. Remember, no matter who or what people say that you are, the only word that matters concerning you is God's Word. Develop thick skin— you're going to need it. You don't want to live in a constant state of offense, since it births bitterness, which blocks productivity and keeps the train derailed.

Reflection: *Identity Theft*

Often, after we've experienced a *destiny derailment,* we will also encounter a season of identity theft. Identity theft can also happen in the aftermath of situations that were beyond our control. Consider your response in a potential identity theft situation, or better yet—what is God's desired response for you? What would you do if you posted a picture or statement on social media and several people began mocking you or identifying you by a condition or something that you wanted to conceal from the world? Marinate on it for a few, consider God's desired outcome for the situation, and then write your response below.

_____

_____

_____

_____

_____

_____

_____

_____

DESTINY DERAILED

Chapter 5: *Redirected by Rejection*

Many times, God uses rejection to isolate us for self-reflection and so that He can clearly deal with us and speak concerning the future. Bishop Jakes advised me to remove myself from the spotlight to spend time with God. Although the Holy Spirit was guiding me in this direction, I was fueled by my flesh for some time after this incident and I continued to check in with social media and concern myself with the opinions of others. Naturally, my inclination was to see what people were saying about me. The spotlight had become my comfortable place. However, in this new reality, the limelight and embracing what came with gospel music, the one place that had once been my comfort zone, now felt like a battleground. I was highly uncomfortable as a result of the rejection I was feeling. I had become so used to having a crowd around me, telling me how wonderful I was and giving me whatever I needed. I had never really dealt with people not accepting me or wanting me around. After the arrest, I honestly felt like a leper.

The Life of a Leper

During biblical times, leprosy was the equivalent of defilement and uncleanliness. In both the Old and New Testaments, lepers were considered outcasts. People couldn't openly associate with them.

My ministry engagements and performances diminished. I was separated from my children, and every show was cancelled except for one. Life went from a calendar that was completely booked with more dates than

I could handle to one single engagement remaining. One-by-one, the calls came in that venues, promoters, and event planners were cancelling my contracts. As I wrote earlier in this book, churches rejected me, and a home-town congregation banned me from their worship service. The pastor's exact words were, "We don't allow felons at our church." When I look back on this, it's really absurd to me. So-called "felons," the people who have been through stuff and want to know God are exactly the type of people that this pastor should have welcomed into his church. Jesus Himself said, *"I have come to call sinners to turn from their sins, not to spend my time with those who think they are already good enough"* (Luke 5:32 NIV). I guess it was a popular and more widely accepted decision to reject me. Besides, the media, the public, and now even the church rejected me. To these people, I fell out of God's grace and I was unworthy of their love, forgiveness, and rehabili-tation. Perhaps it would have shamed and embarrassed the church too much to allow me, a sinner, into their worship services. It would have looked bad. This is nothing new. People who are obsessed with religion, rather than the love of God, always care more about appearances than a man's heart. What things look like matter more to them than participating in God's plan to redeem the earth through the repentance of sinners. Pharisees and scribes disapproved of Jesus fellowshipping with tax-collectors and promiscuous women. I digress.

During this time, rejection became my reality. For years, I had been a reliable shoulder to lean on for so many people and music had been my connection to those who were dealing with difficult situations. Because of my own testimony and the various songs I had written, I was always the one who people came to for advice and support. However, during this time, all that changed. To experience so many people turning their backs on me when I thought I really needed them—be it pastors, churches, the gospel industry, or my friends, and on top of that, dealing with cancellations, loss of income, and isolation—rejection became a reality and it was the most difficult experience that I encountered. The wounds of rejection were deep because they caught me off guard. I did not expect for people to be okay with what happened, but I did expect people to hear me out, accept my flaws, and forgive me. That didn't happen. The lack of support, love, and restoration that I experienced affected me deeply. I'm not sure if we can ever prepare ourselves for rejection. How can we fortify ourselves to be shut out, boxed in, closed off, and unwelcomed from someone, something, or someplace when our deepest desire is to belong?

Rejection is a real evil that has sadly become the reality for many people that we encounter each day, and often we don't know it until it is too late. I would venture to suggest that rejection is the root cause of many murders, suicides, and mass shootings, which have become too popular among our young people. According to the Gun Violence Archive, a national non-profit organization, there have been fifty-seven mass shootings in America this year (2018). On March 20, 2018, there was a school shooting in St. Mary's County, Maryland at Great Mills High School. News outlets reported that seventeen-year-old Austin Wyatt Rollins came to school and shot sixteen-year-old Jaelynn Willey in the head and fourteen-year-old Desmond Barnes in the leg. Apparently, the shooter had a prior relationship with Willey. Both teens who were shot ultimately died as a result of this incident. Rejection probably fueled Austin's anger and prompted him to walk into the school building on that rainy Tuesday morning to shoot someone who he had once cared for. We must figure out ways to help our society cope with disappointment, anger, rejection, and other emotions. We often discuss gun laws and policies concerning the right to bear arms, yet we ignore the underlying issue—our nation is suffering from deeply embedded mental hurts and pains. Rejection seeps into the hearts of many people pushing them over the edge and making them believe the only way out is to die and take others with them. People of all ages are suffering from rejection and fail to receive the proper help to manage these emotions.

Social Rejection

I didn't realize it yet, but I was dealing with what is known as social rejection. This is when an individual is deliberately excluded from social interactions. I would also suggest an expanded definition to include when an individual is treated negatively in social settings. Psychologists and researchers have found that this type of rejection is just as painful and damaging as physical injuries. When a love interest rejects us, when we are fired from a job, when family members don't acknowledge us, or someone is excommunicated from the society he knows, these scenarios are considered social rejection and are triggers for much more serious issues. Several reports have come out in recent years that have scientifically explained why this type of rejection immediately alters our moods and affects our brains in harmful ways.

In short, research has shown that our brains are wired to respond to rejection negatively and similarly to how they respond to physical injuries. When scientists placed people in functional MRI machines and asked them to recall a recent rejection, they found that the same areas of our brains become activated when we experience rejection as when we experience physical pain. That's why even small rejections hurt more than we think they should, since they elicit literal (albeit, emotional) pain.[4] Evolutionary psychologists contribute this to primitive societies when communal economy and living were a way of life. Community was synonymous with livelihood and isolation was considered a death sentence. For those with a Christian worldview, however, we can think of this in terms of creation. God created us to live in community with one another. From the beginning of time, isolation has caused problems for us humans. Look at what happened when Eve was by herself in the Garden of Eden. After God made the heavens and earth, He made man, and He looked at man and said that it wasn't good for man to be alone, that man needed a helper as his partner. In Genesis 2:21, God put man to sleep and formed woman from his rib. We, as humans, were not meant to live alone. We were designed for community, and any existence outside of God's original design triggers an emotional response within us.

Isolation can Lead to Delusion

In Chapter 2, I mentioned the story of Elijah and Jezebel. In 1 Kings 18, Elijah won a major victory for the Lord, defeating 450 false prophets of Baal. In the next chapter, however, we meet Elijah running from Queen Jezebel, hiding in a cave, and asking God to die. Verse three in 1 Kings 19 tells us that Elijah was afraid. After God used Elijah to prove that he was an accepted prophet of God's, Elijah should have been celebrating. Think about it. Not only did his victory glorify God, and discredit the enemy, but it influenced more people to believe in God. Elijah's actions probably had positive effects for generations. Elijah did not celebrate for long or take a victory lap. Instead, he allowed the rejection he received from Queen Jezebel to push him into a state of panic, which prompted fear within his heart. He then isolated himself and drove himself into an even deeper state of worry, fear, and depression. There is a pivotal moment in this chapter where I believe Elijah's story could have went down a more positive path. You see, Elijah was not alone at first. I mentioned this earlier, but it's worth another look; verse three tells us that Elijah left his servant in Beersheba, while he continued a day's journey (alone) into the wilderness.

Now perhaps if he were not alone by himself in the woods for a day, he would not have lost his grip on reality. Rejection and isolation essentially drove the man of God into a suicidal state, but not only that, Elijah lost his grip on reality. Elijah had isolated himself mentally and physically. He reached a cave and finally called out to God in a rejected and dejected state. By this time, he was delusional, and probably delirious as well from a lack of food. When he fell asleep, an angel woke him and said, "Arise and eat" (Verses 5 and 7). Once he ate, he had enough strength to begin his forty days of travel. In verse 10 we learn that due to the isolation he experienced, Elijah thought he was the only prophet left who was on the Lord's side. He thought that Queen Jezebel had made good on her promise and killed all of his counterparts. This moment resonates with me, and perhaps you as well. As I read it, I can feel Elijah's pain. We've all been there— feeling alone because we don't see anyone else fighting for us or with us. Rejection can feel like the end. However, I am reminded through this story that God always has more grace, and, as His children, we are covered. His Word is true that He will never leave or forsake us. After God shares His plans for Elisha to take Elijah's mantle, God tells the prophet, "I have reserved seven thousand in Israel, all whose knees have not bowed to Baal, and every mouth that has not kissed him." One of the lessons that I take from this is that we are never alone, although isolation and rejection can make it seem like we are. When you've been rejected, fight the natural urge to isolate yourself. Cutting yourself off from the world can make you lose a grip on reality. While you are in a derailed state, work hard to remain connected to the body. Don't wander into the wilderness alone.

Feelings of rejection can affect your self-esteem, mood, and if left untreated, those feelings will likely surface in the form of aggression and anger. The rejected person feels like they do not belong and so they lash out. As I mentioned earlier, in recent years in America, we have seen this play out so often in the form of school massacres, mass shootings, or more silently, suicide and chronic depression. People are going to extremes to escape the feeling of rejection, including taking their own and others' lives.

What's very interesting about all of the studies relating to rejection is that not only is emotional pain from rejection comparable to physical pains from cuts or headaches, but in one study, researchers gave Tylenol to a group who had recently experienced rejection. The active ingredient in Tylenol (acetaminophen) seemed to dull the pain from rejection because it dimmed activity in regions of the brain that process social pain. In other words, the same drugs that can treat physical pain can essentially treat emotional pains.

Most people that I know, however, do not consider taking Tylenol for a broken heart, hurt feelings, or to cure the pain of a *Destiny Derailed*. I am curious whether it will actually work so if you decide to try it, send me a message on Instagram and let me know your results. For the group of people who aren't taking an over-the-counter pain reliever for a *Destiny*

Derailed, we have to heal the old-fashioned way. And unfortunately, to all of my old-school saints, "the Christian way," of going to church and laying it on the altar does not work for people who are banned from church or whose own depression and rejection keeps them from the house of God. Sometimes, church people are mean, and those in need of love experience the most condemnation in the church. I personally needed intimate one-on-one time with God without the criticism of church people. There were obviously some proactive steps that I took once I entered therapy that helped me deal with the rejection that I felt, but going to church was not one of them.

I was isolated and felt ostracized from the church. I was not in a place where I could mentally walk into a church and confide in a pastor or be fed by a preacher on a regular basis. I, like many people reading this book, experienced church hurt. Church hurt is one form of rejection that hurts so deeply, since churches are like hospitals, places where we should be able to turn for healing from emotional pain and life crises. The opposite is often true, however. The sad reality of our day is that many local churches have been overtaken by a spirit of religion that judges, condemns, and bans those who've made mistakes and who need the most love and care. Or worse, leaders of the church have abused members of their congregations. We hear stories of sexual, verbal, and spiritual abuse, manipulation, and witchcraft overtaking many congregations, which is a shame.

There are people whose gifts are rejected in the church, or who are criticized for going after their dreams of singing or ministering simply because of jealous church people. Church hurt can come in many forms and fashions, and there is no easy prescription to cure those who've been victimized by church people and leaders. Church was the last place I wanted to be.

For me, "healing" was not about a church or a pastor, support from a congregation, or early-morning prayer circles. I'm not saying I didn't pray and talk to God and seek prayer from those who I knew had my best interests at heart. My healing from rejection began as a result of one-on-one time with

God and going to therapy. I also repented and made a decision to turn away from the attitudes and circumstances that had led me down a wrong path. I would not have been able to do this had I still been concerned about what was going on around me. I was at a crucial point when I needed to focus on what was going on *inside* of me. After trains are derailed, the owners must also conduct an internal investigation of the accident and dissect the inner workings of the train, railroads, and all of the other components involved in that accident. Life derailments should cause us to deeply examine ourselves as well.

My therapist told me one day, "James, you are going to have to be okay with people never trusting you again." She said, "You can't control people and their opinions of you. You can only control yourself." She went on to say the excessive need to be forgiven or trusted by people is another controlling behavior. "That's what got you in this situation in the first place," she said. When I heard her say this, it was honestly like a light bulb turned on in my brain. I realized that I would never be able to control other people and if they reject or accept me, but I can control James. The only person in the world that I could control was me. Often, we stress out over other people's actions and whether they reject or accept us, how they will respond to something we do or don't do. However, in reality, this is all just a waste of time. We can only control our own emotions, actions, and attitudes. We can choose how we prepare for situations. We can choose how we respond to situations, and we can choose the environments where we go (or don't go). We can control all of these things, but we cannot control the atmosphere itself, nor can we control the people we encounter when we leave our personal comfort zones and enter more public spaces.

So, with not many people to talk to but a few family members and friends, God began to use this season of rejection to isolate me so that He could speak to me clearly with no distractions. I needed to be rejected. As much as it hurt and as painful as it was, this was good for me. Let me reiterate for someone who didn't catch it the first time: often, **God uses rejection to isolate us for self-reflection and so that He can clearly deal with us and speak to us concerning our futures**. If you are in a season of rejection, reflect on what God is working on inside of you and what He's saying to you. When you are trying to get your life back on track after a setback, too many people with too many opinions can make it hard to hear the voice of God. Consider Moses. In Exodus Chapter 2, he witnessed an Egyptian beating a Hebrew, and he grew furious; he too was a Hebrew. Moses killed the Egyptian, hid his body in the sand, but then he learned that people had actually witnessed him commit murder. The Pharaoh sought Moses out to kill him, and in fear, Moses ran and hid in Midian. This was a very long season for Moses, and he was dealing with some serious rejection. He was alone in that foreign land for forty years in a season of preparation when God appeared to him in a burning bush. The moment when God spoke launched Moses into his destiny.

I was so used to having a crowd around me telling me how wonderful I was and being there to do whatever I needed. Finally, with no one there— not even my children—and nobody to build me up and tell me how I was great and amazing, I was finally positioned to be alone with God so that I could tell Him how wonderful He is, despite what I was going through.

Rejection will often birth praise.

Through the pain and hurt, I began to praise God like never before. I thanked Him and worshipped Him for sparing my life, for giving me a beautiful family, for speaking with me, for creating me for a purpose, and for not giving up on me. In those moments, as I praised God, I could hear from Him more clearly. There was no clutter and no comfortable, royal treatment to hide behind. It was like being naked and exposed, yet safe, just like a baby being held by his loving parent.

In Genesis Chapter 29, Jacob is married to two sisters, Leah and Rachel, but the Bible says in verse 30 that, "Jacob loved Rachel more than Leah." Leah indeed felt rejected because her father, Laban, had tricked Jacob into marrying her. She was not the sister that Jacob wanted. So the Bible goes on to tell us that when God saw that Leah was unloved, He also saw her affliction. So He opened up her womb and she became pregnant with a son whom she named Reuben. Leah thought that this child was a guarantee that her husband would love her. Instead, nothing changed. She then became pregnant a second time and named this son Simeon, because once again, she said that God saw she was unloved and with a second son her husband would love her. Again, nothing changed. Leah became pregnant for the third time with another son and named this son Levi, thinking that finally her husband would be attached to her since she'd given him three sons. Still, things between her and Jacob remained the same. She became pregnant a fourth time, but this time after years of rejection and years of feeling unloved and unwanted, she said, "This time I will praise the Lord," so she named this son Judah, which means "praise." Judah was birthed out of rejection, yet his name means praise. Don't miss the revelation in that. Leah finally got it; she finally understood that there was nothing she could do to be accepted or loved by her husband so she turned her attention where it should have been all along, on praising God.

Praise became her priority. She gave glory to the One who never stopped loving her and had never rejected her. This is what I experienced. I came to the reality of rejection, which is that you can't make people accept you, but if you turn your focus away from people and place that focus on praising God, who likes and loves you no matter what, the people who don't like you will no longer matter. When you feel rejected or that no one loves you, always remember God loves you no matter what. Praise Him for that. Nothing can change God's love for you. *"For I am certain that nothing can separate us from his love: neither death nor life, neither angels nor other heavenly rulers or powers, neither the present nor the future, neither the world above nor the world below—there is nothing in all creation that will ever be able to separate us from the love of God which is ours through Christ Jesus our Lord"* (Rom. 8:38-39).

Soon, after God dealt with me about rejection, I started to enjoy being in His presence much more than the presence of people, but I needed to hear God's voice. So as I continued to praise God and tell Him who He was to me, and, in turn, He began to speak back to me and tell me who I was to Him. That exchange meant so much to me since I needed to know that living a life of rejection was not going to be my final destination. God confirmed that for me, and it changed my entire perspective and the healing from being rejected began.

He said, **"Your destiny is not tied to who left you."** That one sentence literally blew me away. God still had plans for me and if *they* left me, that means they aren't a part of my destiny. If they were, they would still be here. In the book of 1 John, verse 2:19 we read, *"They went out from us, but they did not really belong to us. For if they had belonged to us, they would have remained with us; but their going showed that none of them belonged to us."* I don't want you to beg another person to stay in your life. If they want to leave, let them go. Give them the gift of "goodbye." If they 'gon make it without you, you 'gon make it without them. Trust me, I know how it feels to feel like you can't make it without the support and love from certain people. Perhaps you feel as if you need them since you've never had to succeed without them.

But let me remind you of this—you don't need them to get to your destiny. They had their season in your life. God didn't bring those people into your life to determine your destiny, God used them to help fulfill your destiny. They played a role in the production and maybe it was even a big role, but that scene is over. God is always going to be your source, and everyone else will always be resources. The amazing thing about resources is that they will always be available. If the well runs dry on one end, turn around and watch how God will open the floodgates on the other. Never expect Him to provide in the same exact way or manner he has done before, because He is an unpredictable God, and yet this principle of provision does not change. As for those people who are no longer meant to be in your life, close the curtain. Clear the stage, and realize who the real Director of your destiny is. Jesus, is the author and finisher of our faith (Heb. 12:2).

Through the experience of feeling rejected by what seemed like the world, I developed a deeper connection with my savior. Although Jesus never sinned, He experienced rejection by people who had praised him. He even experienced rejection by His disciples, including Peter who was the first disciple to receive the revelation that Jesus was the Messiah. On the cross, Jesus was alone with the exception of two thieves and a crowd of people who chastised Him. It's human nature to think we are alone in our rejection, isolation, mistakes, and sin, but the Lord put Himself in our shoes and became like us, so that ultimately we could become like Him. *For our sake he made him to be sin who knew no sin, so that in him we might become the righteousness of God* (2 Corin. 5:21). He can understand what we're going through. Jesus did not sin, but He became sin for us. He experienced the worst type of rejection ever known to man, and when I put my experience into a perspective that centered around the Jesus experience, I knew that I could get through. He set the example for me and for you.

During destiny derailments, when we are in a state of rejection, it's easy to become so consumed with our own feelings that the world begins to revolve around ourselves and our own feelings, versus God. If this is where you've been or what you're currently living through, allow this rejection and time apart from others to redirect you into a life centered in Christ and a closer relationship with Him. Meditate on the rejection Jesus chose to experience for you and me, and be redirected toward God.

Reflection: *Redirected by Rejection*

Rejection has affected us all at some point. Unfortunately, it attempted to paralyze me, and the way that I overcame it was through God's love, self-love, combined with therapy and various spiritual practices.

After Amtrak and other railway companies experience derailments, they too encounter a season of public rejection, but they never lose sight of their purpose and that their companies are necessary despite their mistakes. Jesus, our Savior experienced deep rejection on His way to the cross. He was even betrayed by one of His disciples for thirty pieces of silver. Each day He was criticized by so-called religious leaders. I'm sure that everyone who was uncomfortable with Jesus' ministry for the three years that He served as an itinerant preacher and miracle worker would have loved for Him to return to His old life as a carpenter, but if He would have turned back, His destiny would not have been fulfilled. Imagine how many people would love for you to return to your old lifestyle and your old ways. How many haters would be happy to see you fall back, seep into a state of depression, and return to the lifestyle that you've left? You can't turn back. Jesus kept His destiny and purpose at the forefront of His mind. His destiny was to save the world of our sins. What do you think your destiny is? How can you keep this in view and stay connected despite the rejection that you may experience after a derailment?

DESTINY DERAILED

Chapter 6: *I Forgive Me*

"...Certain events and circumstances have left me carrying a heavy load of guilt. I believe in Christ and His death on the cross, but in this case my beliefs don't seem to have the power to change my feelings. If you knew my situation, you might understand why. People tell me that I need to 'forgive myself,' but I just laugh when they say that. Who am I to 'forgive myself...'"

Someone sent the above comment to *focusonthefamily.com*, a Christian radio show and media outlet that counsels callers and readers from a biblical perspective. I thought this question was really interesting and extremely REAL! What we *feel* often keeps us from the *truth,* that Jesus paid it all for our sins—however horrible they may be. I've personally had to overcome the feelings that some decisions I've made were unforgivable. I've heard about people who committed murder, or adultery, child abuse, and when they were presented with the gospel, they rejected it, believing that they were unforgivable. When I experienced the derailment and rejection that came with it, I experienced this very real feeling, even though I am a believer— many Christians are stuck not able to forgive themselves or accept Christ's forgiveness due to self-condemnation. The Bible has a lot to say about people like us! If you're in a place where it's hard to forgive yourself, this is the chapter where you let that all go and believe and accept that God still has a plan for your life.

You still have a future even after a failure.

It's time to forgive you!

In the Old Testament, God sent the Prophet Jeremiah to His chosen people to let them know that they were forgiven and that He wanted a relationship with them. Jeremiah 31:34 reads, *"No longer shall they teach one another, or say to each other, "Know the Lord," for they shall all know me, from the least of them to the greatest, says the Lord; for I will forgive their iniquity, and remember their sin no more."*

The Israelites were extremely rebellious, committing among other sins, idolatry—meaning they worshipped false Gods. In the church, that's one that we could call a "big sin." Of course the Lord hated this and the Israelites constantly suffered because of their behavior, but yet and still, He forgave them repeatedly and created a plan to not only rescue them from their sins but to also provide a way for the entire world to become His chosen people and experience benefits that were once only available to Hebrews. That answer was and is Jesus. We see it right here in Romans 5:17, *"For the sin of this one man, Adam, caused death to rule over many. **But even greater is God's wonderful grace** and his gift of righteousness, for all who receive it will live in triumph over sin and death through this one man, Jesus Christ."*

Paul says that regardless of how great the sin, God's grace is GREATER! I can tell you from my own experience that you've done nothing so horrible that grace can't cover. God's grace is always greater than sin, no matter what. Because of Jesus' sacrifice, we are forever forgiven. God forgives us and says that He will remember our sins no more. I love how Psalms 103:12 says it, *"As far as the east is from the west, so far has he removed our transgressions from us."*

If two people were traveling and one person started traveling east and the other person started traveling west, if they never changed directions, they would never run into each other. God is saying that once you're forgiven He removes your sins as far as the east is from the west. That means you never have to run into those sins again. That illustration is a powerful one! How many times has the devil reminded you of your sin or used someone on earth to remind you of them? God not only forgives, He also forgets. So shouldn't we be able to forgive ourselves? The Apostle Paul, who perhaps was the best sinner of all prior to his conversion, could relate to having committed atrocious acts that the world would deem unforgivable. After Paul was saved, I'm sure the knowledge of his previous sins were disgusting and upsetting to him. He persecuted God's children and did so in the name of false religion. He captured Christians and gave them over to the authorities to be killed, and that is exactly what Paul (whose name was still Saul) was in the process of doing when Jesus met him, stopped him in his tracks, and changed his path in Acts Chapter 9. Regardless of his past, however, Paul penned Romans 8:1, *"There is therefore now no condemnation to those who are in Christ Jesus."*

By this time, he had received the revelation that he could forgive himself because God had forgiven him. Paul was a human being just like us, and I believe these encouraging scriptures that He wrote in His letters to the different churches were statements that he told himself when the ugly enemy of self-condemnation and guilt attempted to creep up and paralyze his work for the Lord. He also says that *"if anyone is in Christ, he is a new creation; old things have passed away; behold, all things have become new"* (2 Cor. 5:17). Paul also wrote about forgetting the past—in other words, forgiving himself of his past actions so that he could focus on His purpose in Christ. *"Not that I have already attained, or am already perfected; but I press on, that I may lay hold of that for which Christ Jesus has also laid hold of me. Brethren, I do not count myself to have apprehended; but one thing I do, forgetting those things which are behind and reaching forward to those things which are ahead, I press toward the goal for the prize of the upward call of God in Christ Jesus"* (Phil. 3:12-14).

The apostle then instructed all who would read his letter to have the same mind as him regarding the subject. Even today… if you deal with self-condemnation and an inability to forgive yourself, the Apostle Paul's words are for you. I've learned that we cannot fully move forward with past mistakes constantly on our minds. That would be like driving a Toyota

Corolla with five people inside, yet stopping to pick up more. They won't fit. There would be no room. It would be impossible, and if you tried to squeeze more people inside, you'd risk everyone's safety. You must be empty before you can be filled.

I created a mantra that spoke to my soul. "I Forgive Me. I Forgive Me." Repeating this constantly reminded me to let go of the past mistakes and realize that God paid for my guilt and shame. I had to forgive myself and realize that ALL my debts were cancelled. I made an agreement with myself and God that I would accept His grace, my future, and no longer allow decisions from my past to interfere with my destiny. If God had forgiven me, why wouldn't I forgive myself? I decided to stop holding on to things that God had already forgotten. During the time that God was ministering the "I Forgive Me" message to me, He told me that He still had a future for me. This was music to my ears. If you've been reading up until this point and you too are still dealing with rejection or other remnants of your past actions, I want you to look yourself in the mirror, and tell yourself, "You carried this weight for too long. I forgive me now. I'm letting it go. Dear Past, you won't steal my future anymore."

I embraced what my therapist was teaching me. She said, "James, you can't control people forgiving you. Let go of that need to have power and control over their feelings for you. Of course, you know God forgives based on your word, but you can't make other people forgive you. It's okay to desire forgiveness, but you can't worry about their forgiveness, because you can't make them forgive you," she said. I was already working on the dynamics of domestic violence and my power and control struggles in counseling, and began to forgive myself and heal from that, I stopped caring so much about the opinions of others. It wasn't that I didn't want people to accept me—I am still human—but I was more focused on loving myself.

When the public stopped loving me, I slowly allowed myself to take on their perceptions of me and my self-love diminished also. This is why in hindsight I write so passionately about the identity theft component. I was a victim of identity theft, because I fell into believing what society said about me. I adopted *their* identity of me. It started long before this derailment, however. First, I believed their praises and positive words—I not only believed what people said, but society's affirmation of me had become a part of my reality. When things were good with me, I had been celebrated and I allowed the "love" from society to contribute to the view I had of myself. They thought I was great, so I was great. I had become addicted to the applause of man. It was intoxicating. However, once they changed their views, and the public perception of me became negative, my perception of me became negative. I've learned a major lesson from this. We can never grow too attached to public opinion to a point where it affects how we feel about ourselves. This is a dangerous place to be in. This is the "breaking point." When someone loses their own self value and becomes broken to a point where they believe anything, lose their own power, or can be brain-washed by the powers that be, they are easier to control. The only One that should have that much control over you or me is God. The lack of public acceptance was really killing me on the inside. I had been celebrated for so long, and then suddenly I was in a place where people were saying the most horrible things about me. I had to break their opinions off of me and begin loving myself for who God said that I was.

Before I share the process of embracing self-love with you, let me venture off to say that even when we aren't able to love ourselves, the Bible actually instructs us to love God with all of our hearts, minds, and souls. This was the most important commandment according to Jesus. Sometimes, during moments of deep depression and rejection, the only One we can love is God and by loving God, He will teach us to love ourselves. The process of loving myself, once I accepted that God loved me and gave me grace, began with a hard stop. I stopped focusing on the ugliness of my sin and started understanding the beauty of God's grace. Again, I had to realize that my actions did not define who I am. I came to a realization that I did not have to hate myself or beat myself up. That wasn't helping the situation anyway. I didn't have to view me as a monster or a terrible person. My therapist helped me during this process. I would come into her office and say things like, "I really want to be a better person." She would always say, "James you are already a better person; you just need to make better decisions. You have to forgive yourself." I had to remove the shame, realize that I couldn't control other people's opinions. If this is something you've struggled with, I want you to know that God does not bless you based on the opinions of other people. People's personal grudges against you will not stop God's favor on your life.

As a child of God, you have favor, period. You just have to accept it. Sadly, many believers never realize that they have favor just because of who their Father is. Imagine being the president of a company and hiring your own son to come and work for the business. That son has favor on the job and among other employees, simply because they know he is your son. Now, if the son comes to work and never tells anyone whose child he is, he will be treated like anyone else—not like he is a son of the owners and an heir to the business. This is exactly how it is even today. Children of God's have favor by nature of being joint heirs with Christ, children of God. We don't need anyone else's approval, because our Dad owns this entire world. I believe that this is an important truth that Jesus wanted us to grab ahold of when we read about His ministry on earth. Think about how many times that Jesus healed people despite the negative opinions or mistreatment they received from others.

Remember the man in John Chapter 5 by the pool at Bethesda? He had been sick for thirty-eight years. For all those years he had been sitting by that same pool, probably in the same position waiting for the angels to stir the water so that someone could help him in and he could be healed. However, no one ever showed him any love. No one cared about whether this man ever received his healing. It's safe to say that he didn't have favor in their eyes. Nobody helped him get in the pool nor did they work with him to create a plan so that he could get in the pool first and be healed when the water moved the next time. Nobody cared about this man until Jesus came along. The favor from God trumped the lack of favor from man. Jesus simply asked the man if he wanted to be made well. Not realizing who he had encountered, the man began to explain his situation to Jesus, instead of simply saying yes. "Sir, there is no one to help me get into the pool when the water starts moving. While I am coming to the water, someone else always gets in before me," he said in John 5:7. Every time I read this story and the man's response I feel sad and mad for him. This man saw that the other people near the pool had the power to get in the pool but to also help him, yet they chose not to. He was rejected. This rejection caused him to believe that his healing and restoration depended on whether someone would be able to help him get in the water, which is understandable, since it had for over thirty years. Jesus asked that man a question that day, "Do you want to be well?" Today, Jesus is still asking the same question: "Do you want to be made well?" If your answer is yes, you must forgive yourself and accept God's forgiveness.

I hope you get the point about how much God favors you, but, in case you don't, let me remind you of another moment in Jesus' ministry. While he was on the cross, one of the final acts of redemption that Jesus performed was while He was hanging there with nails in His hands. One of the criminals next to Him on the cross said, "Remember me when you come into your kingdom." This thief received a revelation that the man hanging beside Him wasn't a mere mortal man at all, but He was God. Here we see the heart of Jesus in action. He responded, "Truly I say to you, today you shall be with Me in Paradise." While He was dying, Jesus heard the faith of that thief, and declared that he was saved, restored, forgiven! *God so loved the world, that he gave his only begotten Son, that whosoever believeth in him should not perish, but have everlasting life* (John 3:16).

Everlasting life does not begin at the point of your death. It began when you made the decision to join the family of Christ. Jesus told the thief on the cross, "Today you shall be with me in paradise." He didn't say, "When you die, you will be with me." Jesus was saying that at that moment, he was not only forgiven, but he was restored. His eternal kingdom benefits began that moment. Too bad he waited until he was facing death to meet and acknowledge Jesus. He could have been living with Christ as a part of His kingdom before that. Reminds me of the many people who wait until they are on their deathbeds to make the decision to follow Jesus. They could have lived in God's kingdom on earth. Everlasting life, forgiveness, and many other benefits begin at salvation. That means you received all of the benefits of the cross at the point of your rebirth. One benefit of this favor is forgiveness . By remaining in bondage and refusing to forgive yourself, you are throwing away a major benefit that is associated with your status as a kingdom kid, and that benefit is FREEDOM.

Work on yourself; heal, and accept that this derailment does not have to define you forever. Don't let a bad decision stop your destiny. There is nothing that has happened in your life that God didn't already know about before your destiny was predetermined. That derailment was already factored in long before you met it. God met your evil day before you. You're still on course. You still have a destiny ahead of you. A derailment does not mean a permanent stop. It was just a delay for me, and you too. I want you to get back on your train and continue toward your destination.

When it came down to truly loving myself out of rejection, I prayed, I fasted, I studied the Word of God, and I took therapy and counseling seriously. I stress *seriously,* as many men who are ordered to attend counseling for family violence, blow it off and do not do the work required to really take the healing away from it that they should. Often those men have failed to take responsibility for their actions. Sadly, many abusers—both men and women—act like they were the victims and refuse to accept that they have a problem, and therefore therapy does not rehabilitate them. We can choose, due to pride, to remain the same, or we can choose to humble ourselves and receive the help that is being offered. Part of forgiving myself was admitting that I was wrong and then taking the necessary steps to change. If your destiny has been derailed due to mistakes that you know you've made, I urge you to let go of pride and accept the help that you have access to. This is how you're going to move forward. The honesty that you give yourself will lead to your freedom and forgiveness.

There was not a defining moment when I woke up and said, "Today is the day that I will love and forgive myself." It was a process of releasing what the world was saying about me and accepting what God's Word said about me. What is the world telling you about you? Are those things accurate? Do they line up with what God says about you? If not, I encourage you to release it. Let it go, and spend time with God alone so that you can connect with your true identity.

Release the need to replay a negative situation from your past over and over again in your mind. Don't become a hostage to your past by always reviewing and reliving mistakes. Stop being so critical of yourself. Imagine if there was someone who always criticized you. You would not feel like that person loved you no matter how much they claimed they did, because their actions are not loving toward you. Be sure that the way you treat yourself is loving. Criticism is not love if it's not constructive and will not lead to future improvements. Remember that no one is perfect, if we were, there would be no need for Jesus and no need for forgiveness. I realized that this world is cruel enough to me, and there was no need for me to help it out by beating myself up too. That's a word for you. Think for a moment about how the world has literally tried to crush you.

The times you were teased, rejected, betrayed, lied on, told that you weren't worthy or you wouldn't make it—don't you think those things were painful and cruel enough? Now, for a moment, think about the negative thoughts that you replay in your head. The negative talk that you say to yourself, internally—the self-talk that no one else can hear. For me, it sounded something like this: *no one will ever support you again. You messed up big time. You will never bounce back. You messed up. No one will ever be able to trust you again. You were stupid to do that. You shouldn't have said that, or wrote that. That was a dumb decision. You're an embarrassment to your family. Nobody loves you...* I can go on and on sharing the negative self-speak that I had begun to say to myself. It was toxic and it was abusive. I was now abusing myself.

What's interesting is that the world wants us to believe that this type of self-abuse is the appropriate response to have when we mess up. The world wants us to relive the past. People in this world help us out by constantly replaying and republishing images, or talking about the things that went on "back in the day," during family gatherings, or disagreements. The world may try to force you to relive these moments, and the devil will constantly remind you of the mistakes. He wants you to remember them forever, when God says they are forgotten. God has set up a different system. This system is called grace. Once we realize we are wrong, all we have to do is repent—change our mind—turn around, and that's it. The Lord doesn't tell us to beat ourselves up with the past memories or negative talk. Sure, we need to learn lessons from our mistakes so that we don't repeat them, but we should not meditate on the mistakes. In Philippians 4:8, Paul put it this way, *whatever things are true, whatever things are noble, whatever things are just, whatever things are pure, whatever things are lovely, whatever things are of good report, if there is any virtue and if there is anything praiseworthy—meditate on these things.*

Eventually, as I went through therapy, I decided to live my life in forward motion versus past pity. I had to let it all go. I had to stop reliving the past and stop beating myself up for it too. There is no sense in punishing yourself and poisoning your future for the flaws and failures that God has already forgiven. Don't keep reminding yourself of what could have, should have, or would have been. Forgiving yourself is important, since if you can't forgive yourself, you truly can't love yourself. Forgiving yourself is simply letting go of what you are holding against yourself so that you can move on with God. **Pause for a moment and think about it: what are you holding against yourself?** If God has moved on, shouldn't you do the same? It's time to set a prisoner free and once you forgive yourself, you'll discover that the prisoner was you! God has an Ephesians 3:20 future planned out for you, but you can't have that future you until you forgive the past you.

NOW, it's time to let go. Let go of the past and stop reliving it. You can't undo the past. All you can do is to make today the best day of your life. Letting it go does not mean that you lose a memory of what happened. It means that even though you may still recall your past, you no longer allow that memory to produce the same pain, trauma, and resentment in your future. Let go of the pain and welcome joy and happiness back into your life.

It's time to get free! You've forgiven everyone else, now it's time to forgive the person who needs it most—yourself. I know I know, it's so hard to forgive the person you see in the mirror every day. Maybe you have done something that makes you so mad at yourself now, I get it. Or, perhaps you haven't been able to move past allowing someone in your life who hurt you deeply. I understand that too. If you keep holding on to resentment, guilt, and shame, you've basically held on to toxins. Imagine never using the restroom and having all of that old food, alcohol, candy, and junk food stored in your body. You'd be so toxic on the inside. Now, think about your past and every situation that you can't release. You are spiritually constipated with toxic waste stored inside of you. As long as you keep holding it in, every new thing that God is trying to do in your life won't be effective, because the environment inside of you will be too toxic for His seeds to grow. You will not be able to recognize your blessings since the past has actually caused you to be cursed with a toxic environment caused by spiritual constipation! The cycle won't be broken until you stop condemning yourself for things that the Son has already freed you from.

Let's not waste another day holding on to failures of an old you. You may have failed, but you're not a failure. You may have made a mistake, but your life is not a mistake. You are not what you have done. Have you ever had someone say that they forgive you but then they kept bringing up what they said they forgave you for? God says, "I will forgive your sins and I will remember them no more." That means He's not going to keep bringing your past back up. People do that, but God won't. God has already forgiven you, so now it's time to finally forgive yourself. You can't have a future you until you forgive the old you. Say this and mean it from your heart, "I FORGIVE ME!"

I am not sure if that guy who wrote to *Focus on the Family* ever forgave himself and believed that he was truly forgiven by God, but if I could, I would write him a letter and send him this book. I'd let him know that I can relate to feeling unworthy of forgiveness, but that's the exact reason why Jesus suffered on the cross. Jesus' final act on the cross was to forgive a thief deserving of crucifixion. Through that act, He wanted us all to say those three words, "I forgive me," and more importantly He was saying three words to us, "You are forgiven."

Reflection: *I Forgive Me*

Isn't it amazing that God says that He will forgive us and remember our sins no more? Below, I want you to write some words that come to your mind as you meditate on the statement above that comes from Hebrews 8:12.

_____

_____

_____

_____

If you are a child of God, meaning you have accepted Jesus as your Lord and Savior, God says that He will forget all of your sins, He basically sees you as faultless. That means even your worst sin does not show up on His radar. Remember Paul says God's grace is greater.

If you list out the worst things you've ever done, make sure you put Grace > next to it. He doesn't have a list of naughty things you've done like Santa Claus, and He isn't holding grudges like the person you hurt way back in the day. Considering these facts, how do you think that God views you? Write that below.

_____

_____

_____

_____

Hint: think about your best qualities and multiply that by one hundred—even still, God's perspective of you is much better! That's GRACE!

If you are still having a problem with forgiving yourself or moving past your old mistakes, I recommend getting a piece of paper and writing those issues down. Then, after you've thought about everything that you are having a hard time with, ball up that sheet of paper, burn it, or throw it in the first trash can you see, then take the trash out and put it in the dumpster. Send the past upsets exactly where they need to be!

Chapter 7: *Reclaim your Time*

Even now, declares the LORD, "return to me
With all your heart, with fasting and weeping and mourning."
Rend your heart and not your garments.
Return to the Lord your God,
For he is gracious and compassionate,
Slow to anger and abounding in love, and
He relents from sending calamity.
Who knows He may turn and have pity and leave behind a blessing—"
Joel 2:12-14 (NIV)

Your mind is very much like the lens on a camera—it will see whatever you focus on. So if you only focus on your past failures and flaws that's what you will continue to see. But if you channel your vision to only see the lessons and opportunities that can be gained from your past a brighter future will become clear. Many times when we look at our past, those negative emotions cause us to carry it around like a bag of bricks which slows down our progress and hinders our future success. A key to moving forward is to not only understand your past but to learn from it and leverage it. I want to help you change your perspective concerning your past. Instead of carrying your past I want you to leverage your past. That same bag of bricks that you've been carrying around can be used to build a bridge or tower that will help you reach your future goals, to step into your destiny. If you can do this, you will understand that every "loss" wasn't really a loss at all. A popular saying is "we win some and we lose some," but I beg to differ. I feel that we win some and we learn some, because if you can understand how to use your past to work with you and for you, it won't work against you. There is a lesson that we can pull from every perceived failure that will allow us to become better instead of bitter.

What was once seen as an obstacle holding you back can now become an opportunity for growth and change. It no longer becomes a setback, but a stepping stone to go higher than ever before. That's how you leverage your past and repurpose your pain into power. Imagine how much time you can reclaim if you pull the lessons out of the hard times you've experienced and put those lessons to use. Imagine how many people you could help if you tell your story, or teach about that thing that tried to take you out. Whether your derailment came in the form of a medical complication, divorce, bankruptcy, scandal, job loss, loss of a loved one, or drug addiction, once you've overcome, you can reclaim that time. How can you leverage those experiences to repurpose your pain into power?

Profitable Pain

I remember talking to Bishop William Murphy one afternoon, and I wasn't having a good day. There was so much going on and he had been praying for me. I told him about some of the things that were being said about me in the media and I wanted to get some advice from him on whether or not I should respond to it. Bishop Murphy said something to me that, at the time, didn't make any sense at all. He told me, "It can't hurt you." I was holding the phone in complete silence like, "Huh? I'm in pain. So how could he say, 'It can't hurt you?'"

He repeated, "It can't hurt you; I know you're irritated and frustrated, but it can't hurt you."

"This is already hurting me…a lot. I mean like a whole lot," I thought to myself. I know he could sense that I was unwilling to accept what he was saying to me. It wasn't that I wanted to be combative or to disrespect him, but in that moment I couldn't deny what I was feeling and experiencing, what was right in front of me. This chaos that had become my life was hurting me for sure. What he'd said made no sense to me. And I told him so. Accepting that we would not see eye-to-eye right then, he prayed with me before we got off the phone. While I was appreciative of the Bishop's prayer and time, my day didn't get any better. But the words that he shared with me never left my mind.

Later that night as I was watching television, I landed on a special on The Discovery Channel about how oysters produce pearls. The broadcast began to describe the process that takes place when a pearl is produced. A natural pearl begins its life as a foreign object, such as a parasite or piece of shell that accidentally lodges itself in an oyster's soft inner body where it cannot be expelled. This causes great pain and irritation to the oyster. To ease this irritant, the oyster's body takes defensive action. The oyster begins to secrete a smooth, hard crystalline substance around the irritant in order to protect itself. This substance is called "nacre." As long as the irritant remains within its body, the oyster will continue to secrete nacre around it, layer upon layer. Over time, the irritant will be completely encased by the silky crystalline coatings. And the result, ultimately, is the lovely and lustrous gem called a pearl.

Sometimes the pain that we believe is hurting us is God's way of using pain to help us produce something more valuable than we could have ever imagined. The pain didn't come to hurt you, it came to develop something inside of you that would not have otherwise been produced. If the oyster never experienced the pain and frustration that came from the outside object, it would never produce the beautiful and valuable pearl. Watching that show, I realized what Bishop Murphy was trying to get me to understand. Nothing that I was going through could hurt me because GOD was going to use this uncomfortable season to birth something greater than the pain I was experiencing. God was going to make all things work together for my good. I didn't like the discomfort, but it was necessary. When I considered everything that had happened to me through the lens of the pearl-making process and with fresh perspective, I could look back on various moments when the exact same result occurred in my own life. God allowed me to endure seven months of homelessness to birth "I Trust You," which would change my career forever. God allowed me to be uncomfortable in college, and urged me to leave so that I'd pursue ministry full-time. It all worked out. Each and every time. The rumors and chatter from people could not hurt my destiny in the long run. Romans 8:18 says *I consider that our present sufferings are not worth comparing with the glory that will be revealed in us*. Paul tells us that the pain we are experiencing won't even compare to what God is going to reveal in us.

Many times we don't process the purpose of pain correctly. We usually view pain as something negative that is trying to destroy us or steal our joy instead of trusting the "pain plan" that God had already factored into our lives not for our destruction, but for our development and growth. Many times we are strengthened through pain. I remember my personal trainer telling me that the reason I wasn't getting the results I wanted from my work-outs was because as soon as I would feel pain or exhaustion, I would stop. But in order to see the change in my body and endurance that I wanted, I needed to push through and embrace the pain instead of avoiding it. If it wasn't challenging me, it wouldn't change me. The progress that I wanted to see in my health and fitness was right on the other side of pain. The progress and gain that you can experience from your derailment is right on the other side of that painful experience.

Many times the absence of pain makes us feel that we are moving and growing in the right direction. But God has shown me time and time again that sometimes He sends pain into our lives not only to reveal our weaknesses but to also show us our strengths. You may be saying to yourself, "James, so are you saying that pain is good?" I'm not saying that pain is good or bad. I'm saying that pain is real and if processed correctly, despite what you may have thought or felt that you lost, you can still profit from your pain.

Look to Empower Others

I've always been able to relate and connect with people who are hurting. For many years now, I've been ministering in homeless shelters, hospitals, and prisons. On a regular basis, I've been to Jester Unit Prison in Texas, and I've built solid relationships with some of the men and women there. I've ministered in some of the most dangerous prisons in Texas and it's always so amazing to see these people, many of whom are serving really long sentences, still praising God relentlessly despite their circumstances. Many of the men and their families have written me letters about how my ministry has changed their lives and given them the encouragement to remain hopeful in what would appear to be hopeless situations. The power and presence of God brings joy and hope. One young man, Anthony, entered the penitentiary when he was fifteen-years-old, and served twenty years, was recently released and has become a great friend of mine. Not only that, he also works with me in ministry. Anthony is a prime example of how God can and will redeem the time that we've loss because of derailments. Anthony was serious about inviting the Lord to change his life. God just needs your "yes" in order to begin the redemption process. His desire is to restore each of us into the people He created us to be.

Typically, the men that I minister to at this prison have served several years and are now in a unit for inmates who will be released within two years. In this part of the prison, they encounter a Christian curriculum with biblical teachers and guest speakers who are ministers of the gospel. I've had an opportunity to witness the transforming power of God's Word within many of their lives. I know for a fact that the Word can cut through areas that were seemingly hopeless. God always honors His Word and He actually waits for it to be released on earth and seeks it out to perform it (Jer 1:12). Therefore, I want to encourage you, as you are seeking to redeem the time that has been lost, to begin to confess the Word over your life—and believe it.

In addition to the spiritual components involved in recouping and getting back on track, I've learned that it's truly powerful to remind ourselves of past victories. Remind yourself of how God worked through you before, about the people you've blessed, and tell yourself that He will do it again. In my pain process, I began to remind myself that I had made a true difference in the lives of others. I thought about nearly a dozen times when I traveled up the highways to minister to men in prison and even the connections I've made at church events, concerts, and on social media. As I was reentering society after feeling ostracized, simply knowing that God had a purpose for my life, then and now, gave me confidence. I also recalled the testimonies and letters that I'd received, and I was reminded of my friend Anthony who, even after serving twenty years, God restored him. It's easy to forget how blessed we are and how blessed we've been. It's common to fall into a state of depression after a derailment without taking into account the God who healed and restored you in the past. Think about all that God has done. Keep things into perspective. Once God begins to change the course of your life and sets His redemptive power in place, the mistake will work for your good and sometimes will not even matter at all. Often we stress about things that will not even matter in a week, month, year, or a few years down the road. For those situations that will matter, God still can restore, just like He did with Joseph, the Apostle Paul, and my friend Anthony. I love the fact that we serve a God that can literally reclaim our time, no matter how many months or years pass us.

You've read this far, so I know you can relate to feeling like a derailment was actually the end. It often doesn't seem like the time can be restored at all. It certainly doesn't feel like the future can be brighter, and when our heads are so far down in our derailment, it's natural to think about the time that went down the drain. However, by this point in the book, I hope you're beginning to see a glimmer of hope and the streak of light shining through at the end of your dark tunnel. Prayerfully, you have worked through the rejection and you've identified how God has redirected you despite the lack of approval from people. Have you also accepted that God has given you grace for the situation, despite how you feel? Have you forgiven yourself? You have exhaled the toxic thoughts. You have exhaled the past memories and instant replays of the derailment. You have silenced the naysayers and you've confronted the derailment head-on. If you can shake your head in agreement that you've worked through the past and you've forgiven yourself, you are ready to move forward. You are ready to get your life back on track, back onto the destiny path that God has preordained. You are ready to surrender completely and reclaim your time.

> *"I will repay you for the years the locusts have eaten—*
> *the great locust and the young locust, the other locusts and the*
> *locust swarm—*
> *my great army that I sent among you.*
> *You will have plenty to eat, until you are gull,*
> *And you will praise the name of the Lord your God,*
> *Who has worked wonders for you;*
> *never again will my people be shamed.*

Joel 2:25-26 (NIV)

Healing and restoration take work.

It takes more than reading one book or saying that you're going to change. Change requires a mental shift, a change in thinking, which leads to a change in being (or behavior), and then a change in lifestyle. I went through over three years of counseling. I cannot fully explain how impactful my time in counseling was for me. I hear so many people with so many excuses about why counseling or therapy will not work for them, but I strongly urge every-one who needs it to find the right counselor or group and commit to it.

It is truly a life changer. While in group therapy with ten other men of all different races, backgrounds, and social statuses, I was determined to be different from that point forward. Group therapy was a game changer for me, because we were able to share our experiences, admit our faults, and take accountability for our actions in a non-judgmental environment. This was new for me, since as I mentioned, I had often been praised and affirmed by those around me. Due to the praise from other people, I rarely communicated my faults and verbally expressed my feelings—besides in songs that I wrote—in fear of tainting the image that others had of me. However, in group therapy, I worked through my issues alongside other men who had also been accused of similar crimes. We learned that abuse isn't a mistake—it's a choice. I had time to reflect on the different occasions that I had exerted power and control in my relationship. I also made a conscious decision to avoid those traps again at all costs. During these times of reflection and transparent conversations, God was in the beginning stages of restoring me, from the inside out. By my simple act of obedience (seeking help), I started to reclaim my time without even realizing it. See, it's impossible to reclaim your time if you don't get to the bottom of your mistakes and allow God to restore the deep wounds from the past.

Once the twenty weeks of group therapy was over, I felt a pull from God calling me to become vocal about what had happened. As I went through counseling and started learning about the importance of accountability, I remember God speaking to me about sharing my story to help others. He not only wanted me to speak with men but also to women—to help them understand that they were not at fault for the abuse they experienced. God also wanted me to help others understand the definition of abuse and to share my perspective on how women and men could identify the signs of abuse before it ever becomes physical.

I began to share my story in interviews, and I took complete responsibility for my actions. Then, I responded with a resounding "yes" to requests for me to speak at domestic violence shelters and organizations. At first, I was nervous and uncomfortable with this. I didn't know how I would be received and it was not something that I had considered prior to this prompting from God. However, you probably know that in order to grow, we must be stretched. I continued my inner work in individual therapy and counseling and also anger management. Once that was over, I went through a life coaching program with Dr. Ivan Young. I began to see the importance of this part of my story. I didn't like what happened or who I was at that point in my life, but the new, rehabilitated me wanted to make a difference. I believe God put a fire inside of me to learn more about domestic violence, and He gave me a revelation about how to stop domestic violence before it gets too serious.

I volunteered at several domestic violence shelters and groups. I had an opportunity to listen to several incoming calls to the national hotline from women who were in danger at the hands of an abuser. It was painful to hear their tears and the tremors in their voices from fear. Not only did my heart grieve for abuse victims, but I couldn't help but think about the many children who were traumatized as a result of the violence happening in America. I wanted to hold my children closely. I wanted to tell these women that it wasn't their fault. I wanted to somehow, someway make the resources that I was afforded available to the men who'd lost their cool and abused their wives and girlfriends. I know that all abuse cases aren't men abusing women, but I was exposed to the more traditional cases where the men had exerted power and control over their wives and girlfriends.

In the midst of my therapy and rehabilitation, one of my counselors told me that since I had been an abuser once before, I had a higher risk of becoming abusive again. I didn't want to think about or imagine ever putting anyone else or myself through this a second time. But the truth is that once a person resorts to abuse, there is a higher risk of them doing the same thing again—and again. I've done several interviews where I speak out against abuse, because I've realized that many people do not know what it is. Not only do many abusers not realize that the power, control, emotional and verbal insults are forms of abuse, but many women or victims in these situations aren't aware either. I believe that if more people were educated about the facts of domestic violence and intimate abuse, how to identify it, prevent it, and escape it, relationships would be better off and our country and world would be safer places.

Oftentimes, God's idea of redeeming our time looks much different than what we would expect. I did not think that I would be volunteering in anyone's domestic violence organization. I didn't think that I would be ministering to victims or speaking out against this issue in the media. I never considered myself an abuser, but as I mentioned, my past included threads of power, control, verbal, and emotional abuse. When God redeems our time, we have to be prepared to use the situations that seem completely opposite from what would make logical sense. I thought my life was over, but the entire time, God was positioning me to reclaim my time—first by taking accountability, getting help, being restored from the inside out, and then sharing what God was doing in my life with others. Our purpose and destiny is never only about us. In fact, even when we are the center of attention, God's desire is for our attention to draw attention to Him. Purpose is always about empowering someone else. We are blessed to be a blessing and a major part of reclaiming our time is experiencing God's blessings so that we can bless others. I was blessed to be rehabilitated, to experience healthy counseling experiences, to have a strong support system, and a talent and calling in the kingdom of God. God did not bless me with these experiences and traits for me and me alone. He had major plans to reclaim my time, but it involved me paying it forward.

Remain open to becoming a vessel for change, especially in the areas of your biggest struggle. At the Passover meal, before Jesus was betrayed, He addressed Peter who, along with the other disciples, was caught in an argument about who would be the greatest in Jesus' coming kingdom. The Lord turned to Peter and said, "Simon, Simon, Satan has asked to sift all of you as wheat. But I have prayed for you, Simon, that your faith may not fail. And when you have turned back, strengthen your brothers" (Luke 22:31-32). Jesus was telling Peter that he would go astray, but once he found his way back to his rightful path, his duty would be to strengthen his brothers.

Later on, there was a powerful exchange between Jesus and Peter that was recorded in John 21. Peter had indeed rejected and denied Jesus during the final moments of His life. After Jesus returned following the resurrection, He approached Peter, and asked him three times if Peter loved Him. Peter repeated "yes," and by the third time, he was growing frustrated and probably hurt that Jesus continued to ask. Jesus was preparing Peter for the mission ahead of him. Jesus needed Peter to remember this moment of redemption. He told Peter, "Feed my sheep." With these three words, Jesus instructed Peter to share Christ with others, to pay it forward, and to carry the gospel into the world. Peter accepted his God-given mission and became the leader of the early church, preaching a sermon that would increase the kingdom of God by thousands and usher in the first recorded move of Holy Spirit. Jesus reclaimed Peter's time after His derailment, but Peter had to accept his calling.

Reflection: *Reclaim your Time*

What are your struggle areas? Most likely, God will have you revisit them once you've healed, recognized any fault of your own, and allowed Him to transform you. Think about Peter, one of Jesus' disciples. He boasted about how it was no possible way that he would deny Jesus, and yet the unthinkable happened. Peter had a moment when Jesus was on His way to the cross, where the rooster crowed and he remembered exactly what Jesus had prophesied regarding that moment. Once Jesus rose from the dead, He had a straight talk moment with Peter and told him that if he did in fact love Jesus, he'd need to feed His sheep. This was Peter's moment of rehabilitation, of acceptance. Peter agreed and became a key figure in the early church, preaching the gospel of Jesus Christ at Pentecost, causing 3,000 people to get saved (Acts 2:41).

Don't hide from your past mistakes. Allow God to leverage them so that you can reclaim your time and redeem the promised destiny awaiting you.

Chapter 8: *The Comeback Circle*

On Tuesday, June 18, 2013, the San Antonio Spurs and the Miami Heat were in the NBA Finals for Game Six at the American Airlines Arena in Miami, Florida. The San Antonio Spurs were only twenty-eight seconds away from winning the NBA Championship. They had even rolled the championship trophy to the side of the court so that after the game it could be presented to the Spurs. Everyone in that arena and watching that game all over the world were certain that the Spurs would be world champions. Many of the Heat fans began to walk out of the building, heads hung in disappointment, accepting their team's season appeared to be over. These disloyal fans didn't want to stay around and be there as their team lost. They had been there during the winning season, but now that it was over, they didn't want to stick around and encourage the team through this season-ending lost.

No Reentry

In a matter of moments, during this breathtaking basketball match, LeBron James hit a three-pointer which brought his team within two points. The Spurs then hit a free throw, and then, with one second left in the game, Ray Allen hit a three pointer to tie the game sending it into overtime. At that moment, many of the Heat fans who had left the game tried to get back in, but because of the NBA's strict security policy, which allows no reentry, these fans were not able to get back. News reports showed that it got extremely heated at the entrance doors as fans demanded to be let in and security held their ground.

The Miami Heat went on to win the game in overtime coming back from what seemed like a guaranteed defeat. Not only did they come back and win that game, but they also won the next game and became the 2013 NBA World Champions. The loyal fans who hadn't given up on their team were still in the building and were able to celebrate the victory with their team. They stayed and reaped the reward. The fans who left the game were locked out and forced to watch the victory on the lobby screens through the glass of the building. That's how many people are in your life. As long as you are winning, they are right there cheering you on, telling you how wonderful you are, and bragging about being a part of your team. But as soon as the score changes and it appears that you have lost and your season is over, they find the nearest exit and walk out of your life until your next winning season.

Sometimes you have to have the same policy that the NBA has for its basketball games. "No Reentry."

> # If people can't ride with you during the losses, they don't need to be celebrating with you during the victories.

It doesn't mean that you have to cut them off completely, but they can watch through the glass. When it appears that your season is over, you will find out who your real supporters are. You don't need people celebrating and cheering you on when you're on the mountain top if they can't encourage and pray for you when you're in the valley. Sometimes God will allow it to "appear" that your season is over so that the people who need to exit your life will leave. Don't waste energy focusing on who leaves the stands during the game. You're going to need that energy for the greatest comeback of your life. You are still going to win!

Discovering your Winning Team

In Genesis, God said that it's not good for man to be alone. The original design of God is for us to be in community with one another. God likens His church to a body, and in a body, there are various different parts that keep it all working together as one unit. Imagine if you were missing an eye, a finger, and a knee. You would not be able to operate at your best. The physical body and the body of Christ truly cannot function according to God's original intent and design without all of the parts that He created working as one. This is why in a church, there are some people who preach, others who teach, those who exhort, and others who prophesy or edify the body. You have camera operators, choir members, ushers, children's church directors, intercessors, and so forth. We need each other. There's a team out there that will help you win, and it's key that you connect with those people.

One of the sad consequences for many people who experience some of the issues that we've been addressing in this book such as rejection, church hurt, shame, condemnation, and derailments is that they fall into an isolated state for long periods of time and refrain from reentering the community of God. Do you choose to attend Bedside Baptist rather than a brick and mortar church? Do you have strong relationships with other believers to whom you are accountable? The Word teaches us that iron sharpens iron. We already saw what happened with the prophet Elijah in the Old Testament when there was no one there to keep him sharp. God has equipped other believers with the answers we need.

As flawed as it may be, the church is the body of Christ and the community of God, and every believer is necessary in that community. There are many believers who, after being hurt, choose to fall back from the church (as in the body of Christ) or life in general. I've been there, and I completely understand the desire to worship on one's own, pray, and build a relationship with God by oneself, but that is just not the way God intended life to be forever. If I would have allowed the shame, hurt, anger, and embarrassment from this derailment to keep me isolated and away from the community that God has assigned to me, I would not have been living God's designed plan for my life, and I would have been depriving others the ministry that God put into me. There will be seasons (as we've discussed) in which it will benefit you to get alone with God, but that is not how it's supposed to be forever. Not only will the community of God often help you come back stronger than ever, but you also bless the Body. You need them, and the community needs you as well.

Adam needed Eve to be his helpmate, and Eve needed Adam to lead her and to help her resist the devil's temptation to eat from the tree of the knowledge of good and evil. Adam was not beside her during that moment of weakness and we see what happened as a result. Amos 3:3 asks, "Can two walk together, except they be agreed?" The answer is "no." The power of agreement when there are two or more people working together is a super force and another important reason for community. Jesus tells us this in Matthew 18:19, "Again I say to you that if two of you agree on earth concerning anything that they ask, it will be done for them by My Father in heaven." Godly agreement, companionship, help, and support are some of the reasons why God created us to operate within a circle of other believers.

There would be nothing spectacular about a one-person church, a one-person concert, a one-person school, a one-person movie, or a one-person basketball game. Even Jesus Christ Himself knew that in order to carry out God's purpose for the world, He'd need disciples, apostles, evangelists, those who serve, and so forth. There were always crowds around Jesus, He worked in ministry with a group of twelve, and He had an inner circle of three. The only times we see Him alone is when He first began His ministry and He was in the wilderness for forty days. At other times He was alone only when He prayed, or slept. If we model our lives after our Savior's, we can get a clear picture of the importance of community in carrying out our God-given ministries—and yes, everyone has one. We cannot live alone. We all need a circle of friends, a community—be it big or small—to carry out God's purposes for our lives.

Given this truth, let's look at what happens when our inner communities don't function properly. What happens when you find that the people in your circle are not supportive to the overall mission God has for your life? As time wound down in Jesus' ministry, the one person who did not support His life's mission was close enough to kiss him. It was Judas, who betrayed Jesus and turned Him over to the Roman authorities to be crucified. (This however, was a part of the overall purpose for the world and it actually fulfilled previous prophetic scriptures about the Messiah. Still, the closeness of Judas to Jesus and how that came into play with the crucifixion is the point I am making here.)

After a derailment, we've already discussed that God's desire is to build you up and restore you to complete wholeness. After you've dealt with the self-guilt and doubt and are able to trust God again, it's time for your life to experience a resurrection. Your circle during and after the derailment is critical to your comeback. Once again, think about the apostles' roles in Jesus' mission once He arose from the grave. Had He not had them around during that critical time, the gospel would not have spread. If there were no one to share "the good news" that Jesus rose from the grave, who would have believed that it actually happened? Although Jesus died to save the world, if it weren't for the disciples and the women who returned to His grave that Sunday morning to witness an empty tomb no one would have been there to witness to others. Jesus didn't just choose anyone to witness His resurrection, either. He chose the right people.

See, there could have been Pharisees or Roman soldiers there, who would have no doubt kept silent about the miracle they had witnessed. Instead, Jesus made sure that His most devoted were there. The first person He appeared to was Mary Magdalene. This is the same Mary who Jesus had healed of seven demons. She was a devoted follower and friend of His after that. She cared for Him, and she would surely spread the word about His resurrection. There will be people who will see what God is doing and has done in your life, believe your vision, and share it with the masses. God is strategically placing the right people in your path. You won't have to do all the work alone.

Let's back up for a moment to the point when you derailed. Are you are ready to move forward? Who are the people around you? Let's look at how they can make or break you. As I was thinking about this concept, the book of Job in the Old Testament came to mind. Job 2:11 reads, "When Job's three friends, Eliphaz the Temanite, Bildad the Shuhite, and Zophar the Naamathite, heard about all the troubles that had come upon him, they set out from their homes and met together by agreement to go and sympathize with him and comfort him." Did you catch that? Job's boys knew he was in distress, left their individual homes, and *came into agreement* to be there for him. They went to meet with him and comfort him. Job had been a man of great influence and even a person who encouraged and strengthened others during their times of need (Chapter 4:3-4). Despite him being extremely popular, giving, supportive, and kind to others, when he was experiencing adversity, his circle of friends was reduced to three people. Isn't his situation so telling, even of the times we live in today? When everything was going great in his life and when he had influence and power, everyone wanted to be around him. Everyone wanted to be close to him, and all of these people wanted something from him. But when he was stripped of everything, with nothing left to give, the people were no longer interested in being connected to him. I can certainly relate to that!

I've learned that we never really know who our real friends are until we go through storms. When you are on the mountain, everyone wants to be with you and say they know you, but when you go through a valley, it can be a very lonely walk. People can sometimes be no different than shadows. They stick around during our brightest moments, but during our darkest hours, they disappear. The Bible says in Job Chapter 2 that his three friends sat with him for seven days and seven nights. It's easy to find friends who will stay with you for the seven days, but it's often a challenge to find friends who will be there for the seven nights—the darkest moments. During my derailment, God helped me to understand that I had to be very careful who I let around me during that season. He told me that my circle during this crisis would be critical to my survival. Everyone wants to give advice and their opinions, but bad advice can lead to an extended season of derailment. We see that even in Job's life. Although his friends were around, the three in question became negative and gave him bad advice—the same is true for his wife who in Chapter 2, verse 9 said, "Do you still hold fast your integrity? Curse God and die."

If you can just imagine for one moment the whirlwind my life had become. The calls came from everywhere—media, the record label, and people that I'd connected with from all over the country. Everyone had an opinion about what I needed to do in order to minimize the impact of the derailment. Had I been quick to respond in haste to any of these suggestions, I would have been like a yo-yo, going up and down, up and down, and I would have made the situation much worse. (Remember Philippians 4:6-7, *"Do not be anxious about anything, but in every situation, by prayer and petition, with thanksgiving, present your requests to God. And the peace of God, which transcends all understanding, will guard your hearts and your minds in Christ Jesus."*) I desperately needed God's peace with my decisions. I've learned that when we're in trouble and people come to us with advice that seems good and well, it's best to slow down and not respond to it immediately. Sometimes the responses are outward actions or steps that can remedy or worsen the situation, and at other times, the responses are mental, as in accepting a viewpoint or mentally agreeing with someone else's position, which can have a significant impact on us (and less often, them). It's important to have people in your corner who will avoid being negative, judgmental, or even too talkative. What helps most during a derailment is sound advice or people who are willing to simply listen.

There is a way that seems right to a man,
But its end is the way of death.

-Proverbs 14:12

The Bible repeatedly warns us to be careful of the company we keep. The wrong influences often point us in the wrong direction. What we learn, or are told, by the wrong persons (or those with limited perception or insight into the situations) can direct us into making wrong decisions that we may regret. I had to pray and really reevaluate many of my friendships and relationships. One of the ways I did this was by paying close attention to the words and actions of people around me during this season. Words reveal heart motives, and I immediately questioned the motives of people who were hitting me up just to find out information or to see what parts of the story were true and untrue. I also limited interactions with people who called to gossip and tell me the latest information being publicized in the media. I didn't need that either. Receiving hour-by-hour or day-by-day commentary on what the press and social media were talking about as it pertained to my situation just reminded me of how bad things had become. The total opposite is what we need during times like this. It was obvious that the situation was bad, but I needed to believe that it would get better. I needed hope—not worry and anxiety.

When Job's friends came to him they sat with him for seven days and nights, at first, they just wanted him to know that they were there. When the men got their first glimpse of him, they barely recognized him and knew by the looks of him that his suffering was very intense. When you are going through serious pain, you don't need people around you who are not there to comfort you. It's difficult enough dealing with yourself; you don't need anyone making you feel worse than you already do. You need people who you can be vulnerable around, people that do not require you to become an actor or actress and play a role like you're stronger than you actually are. You need to be able to be honest and say that, "I'm not okay right now." It's fine to be emotionally honest with yourself and admit that you're afraid or that you're tired of pretending to be strong. God's strength is not made perfect in our strength; it's made perfect in our weakness.

I was tired of putting on for people, and I needed to strip off the mask and deal with the man inside of me. I needed to cry. I needed to be able to say, "I don't think I can make it through this." I needed people around who wouldn't judge me for being human. So my circle became extremely small. My mom and sister would meet with me daily to encourage me and let me know that my current condition was not going to be my final conclusion. I knew that they were hurting too, but they were there to be strong for me because I was dying on the inside. Their words to me were powerful, but their presence was so valuable, often conveying silent strength. I didn't want to be out in public. It seemed like the whole world was against me, so my family made sure that I didn't have to be alone. We would enjoy each other's company and spend time laughing, talking, and sometimes, for a brief moment, I would actually forget about the pain I was experiencing especially from not being able to see my children. I could not have lived through that season without them.

I moved in with my dad, and one day he shared something that I really needed to hear. He said, "They can take your job and they can take material possessions from you, but they can't take your gift. You can survive this." He was right. Every good and perfect gift comes from above (James 1:17). God had given me the gifts of music, ministry, and even life, and He was not an Indian giver. One of my best friends, Isaac Carree, called me every single day to check on me and make sure that I was okay. But one day he called and before I could say a word, he just began to weep on the phone. He had been so strong for me for so many days during this process, but on that day he finally broke. He was hurting not because of his own circumstances, but he knew that what I was experiencing was so intense that my pain had penetrated his spirit and like Job's friends in Chapter 2 verse 12, he began to weep out loud. This touched me in such an impactful way.

Even though I had been trying to mask my misery and act like what was happening on the outside was not affecting me on the inside, Isaac knew better. His transparency and vulnerability opened me up and allowed me to take off my hard exterior so that he could encourage me from an honest and real place. I could trust him with my true feelings. That's what you need during a crisis. You need people around you who you can be completely open and honest with. Suppressing those feelings and stuffing away issues only makes them worse. Sometimes we need to vent or vomit. We need to get those toxic feelings and thoughts out of our spirits so that we can experience healing and wholeness. What my derailment taught me about my circle during a crisis is that it's less important to have a lot of people in my circle, and more important to have the *right* people in my circle—people who will uplift and encourage me the way Paul encouraged the church at Ephesus when he reminded them of the hope they had in God despite their present predicament. *"I keep asking that the God of our Lord Jesus Christ, the glorious Father, may give you the Spirit of wisdom and revelation, so that you may know Him better. I pray also that the eyes of your heart may be enlightened in order that you may know the hope to which He has called you, the riches of His glorious inheritance in the saints, and His incomparably great power for us who believe"* (Eph. 1:17-19).

Eventually, as Job continued to lament, his friends also became more talkative and less supportive. No one could understand why Job had experienced such tragedy, and they began to accuse him. First, Job's friend, Bildad, encouraged him to repent (Chapter 8). Then, Zophar took a self-righteous stand, and told Job that he didn't even receive half of the punishment that he deserved and that he lacked wisdom (Chapter 11). Eliphaz accused him of not fearing God (Chapter 15). By the time we get to Chapter 16, Job had enough of his so-called friends,

"I have heard many such things;
miserable comforters are you all.
Shall windy words have an end?
Or what provokes you that you answer?

I also could speak as you do,
if you were in my place;
I could join words together against you
and shake my head at you.
I could strengthen you with my mouth,
and the solace of my lips would assuage your pain. "

Job 16:2-5

Job and the men went back and forth for almost twenty more chapters, with Job sinking deeper and deeper into pity and his friends growing less and less compassionate of his situation. Their position was that Job suffered due to sin, however Job continued to withhold his theories and told them that often the wicked did prosper. It got to a point where they no longer had any answers for him, yet the long conversations still had not solved Job's problems. I imagine that this greatly confused Job, and his friends' mistrust and blaming simply piled onto the distress that he must've felt. They started off supporting him, yet with time, as his derailment continued, they grew more impatient, accusatory, and less loving. In Job Chapter 32, a younger guy, Elihu, who must have been watching and listening to this entire ordeal, rebuked Job's friends and offered a new perspective on Job's suffering. As the website *desiringgod.com* described… "here we learn something that neither Job nor his friends had discovered, namely, that the suffering of the righteous is not a token of God's enmity but of his love. It is not a punishment of their sins but a refinement of their righteousness. It is not a preparation for destruction, but a protection from destruction. The three friends have been wrong—suffering is not the proof of wickedness. And Job had been wrong—his suffering was not the proof of God's arbitrariness. Nor had God become his enemy. Elihu has come to put the argument on a new footing." There are many perspectives of Elihu's rebuttal to Job and his friends, however, what I appreciate most about Elihu's speeches is that they begin by explaining that Elihu was disappointed with Job because he attempted to justify himself, rather than God.

At the end, when the Lord appeared and began to speak with Job, he is moved to repentance for some of his words. God also rebuked Job's friends in Chapter 42:7-8, *"After the LORD had spoken these words to Job, the LORD said to Eliphaz the Temanite: "My anger burns against you and against your two friends, for you have not spoken of me what is right, as my servant Job has. Now therefore take seven bulls and seven rams and go to my servant Job and offer up a burnt offering for yourselves. And my servant Job shall pray for you, for I will accept his prayer not to deal with you according to your folly. For you have not spoken of me what is right, as my servant Job has."*

After Job prayed for his fair-weather friends, God restored Job's fortunes with twice as much as he had before. There are so many lessons that we can take from this book of the Bible regarding friendships during a derailment. I pray that you see the importance of a strong, loyal circle. When we have people who cannot remain in faith (as was the case with Job's friends), they can tend to justify wrong situations (and responses) by their own thoughts and feelings instead of what the Word tells us. My circle diminished and that was for my good. Once you realize who is there for you during hard times, stick close to them. God sent them to you for a reason and purpose. Take them with you in your next season of restoration, when God restores all that you lost and more.

Reflection: *The Comeback Circle*

While you're getting your life back on track after a derailment, you are at your most vulnerable state. It's easy to fall prey to everyone else's opinions of your situation, verses staying focused. Gossip and reports of what *he* or *she* are saying will only distract and discourage you. Bad news period will become discouraging blocks that you will have to get over. The best way to forge ahead is to take a page from the classic movie *The Wiz*, and accept **NO BAD NEWS.** This will be impossible to stick to if you have negative or unhealthy people around you. Those within your Comeback Circle need to have strong faith and be focused on empowering and listening to you. They need to be able to see the light at the end of your tunnel and encourage you with positive words of wisdom or no words at all. Sometimes, the people closest to us, including immediate family members, are not people who should be walking through derailments with us. Perhaps they can come back on the train once you're moving again, but while you're in that critical stage of maintenance when God is re-engineering your course, you cannot afford to have their negative outlook and output.

Take a moment to reflect on the people in your circle. Even if you're not experiencing a derailment right now, it's wise to check your crew before something detrimental hits to make sure that you have the right people around you. If not, make adjustments before you go through the next setback. Pay close attention to what people say and pray and ask God to give you the ability to discern the motives of their hearts.

DESTINY DERAILED

Chapter 9: *All Things New*

It's not over,
It's not finished,
It's not ending,
It's only the beginning,
When God is in it,
All things are new…

- Israel Houghton

In 2012, Israel Houghton invited me to record a song with him for his up-coming *Jesus at the Center* album, released in August of that year. The song, "It's Not Over (When God is In It)" repeats the affirmation, "When God is in it, there is no limit. When God is in it, it's not over." The message behind the song is so simple, and it's one I'd return to years later – that God makes all things new. The song is a beautiful and powerful reminder that life isn't always what it appears to be. Although our situations appear to be hopeless, God's nature is synonymous with hope. When God is in it, (or in us), it's not over. He can and will make all things new.

In reality, what I experienced was hard for human hearts to accept and reconcile. For so long, I even had a hard time accepting me and that my career was on the rocks, that I could not see my children for seven months, and my marriage had ended publicly. However, my problems—your problems—are no match for God, the master of restoration. In my life, God had already begun to reconstruct a comeback, a new beginning that I could not yet see. God is experienced in rearranging broken pieces into master-pieces. He is indeed the author of new, and all He needs is our "yes." I sure do hope that at this point in the book, you've given God your yes. I pray that you've let go of the old mistakes and past failures. I want you to embrace the new.

Here's what the Word says. Allow these verses to sink into your spirit. Meditate on them and allow them to minister to your broken places—your old places, the places that you haven't wanted to touch or uncover. God wants to shine light there too. He even wants to make those places new:

Remember not the former things,
nor consider the things of old.
Isaiah 43:18

Behold, I am doing a new thing;
now it springs forth, do you not perceive it?
I will make a way in the wilderness
and rivers in the desert.
-Isaiah 43:19

For behold, I create new heavens
and a new earth,
and the former things shall not be remembered
or come into mind.
Isaiah 65:17

You were taught, with regard to your former way of life, to put off your old
self, which is being corrupted by its deceitful desires; to be made new in
the attitude of your minds; and to put on the new self, created to be like
God in true righteousness and holiness.
Ephesians 4:22-24

In speaking of a new covenant, he makes the first one obsolete. And what
is becoming obsolete and growing old is ready to vanish away.
Hebrews 8:13

But why?

Although truthful and encouraging, "God will make all things new," has become a Christian cliché, but have you ever thought about why? Why will God make all things new? He has given us so many promises of hope, and that everything will work out, but have you ever thought about why? Yes we are His children; yes we are joint heirs with Christ, but even still, why does He promise us provision, companionship, and new life, a resurrection? The answer can be found in Psalm 72:19, *"Blessed be his glorious name forever; may the whole earth be filled with his glory!* or Isaiah 42:8 *"I am the Lord; that is my name! I will not yield my glory to another or my praise to idols."* or Habakkuk 2:14, *"For the earth will be filled with the knowledge of the glory of the Lord as the waters cover the sea."*

> ## We win because He gets the glory.

And when God is glorified, people are redeemed from the grips of hell and the pits of darkness and thrust into the light. When God makes us win, He wins. When we are redeemed, God is revealed. When we defeat Satan, truly, what has occurred is a victory for God. This is why in 2 Chronicles 20:15, the Spirit of the Lord affirmed to King Jehoshaphat not to fear the Ammonites or the Moabites. He said, *"Do not be afraid nor dismayed because of this great multitude, for the battle is not yours, but God's..."* The battle that you are fighting is God's. He will get the glory and He will give you a fresh start after what appears to be a dead end.

137

***

One of the attributes of Christ that I love the most is that He will break all of the rules to make us completely new. He does not care who does not approve. He does not need to be validated. He does not care about the usher who has condemned you to hell, the pastor who kicked you out of his church building, the ex who bashed you on social media or the job that fired you. When He's ready, He will give you that big promotion you've been praying for in the same company and in the presence of the same boss who low-balled you last season. He is God, and He is the author of new. God not only needs NO permission whatsoever, but He doesn't care about our frivolous plans, worldly calendars, biological clocks, or manmade timelines. He doesn't care what anyone says, and He doesn't require us to be "qualified" for the blessings that He plans to bestow on us. The world and our four seasons are on Chronos time, meaning seconds-minutes-hours-days-weeks-months-years. However, God is on Kairos time. Kairos is a Greek word meaning "opportune, right, or critical" time. That's right, essentially "perfect timing." If you've ever wondered why God is taking so long to answer a prayer of yours, you need to take a step back and realize that God literally is not on your time. Kairos time is governing your destiny, your comeback, and your new season. That means that at just the right time, at the critical and opportune time, you're going to birth that ministry, meet the man or woman of your dreams, receive the opportunity you've been searching for. At the opportune time, God is going to make all things new.

God is also unpredictable and quite original. As I've observed my life, the lives of others and even the biblical stories that we have as examples, I realize that I have never seen God bless two people in the same exact way and manner. He is unpredictable and the Lord of creativity. Often, He changes His methods so that we don't get so caught up in the method that we miss the Messiah. In John Chapter 9:1-12, a man had been blind since birth. Jesus spat on the ground, made some mud, put it on the man's eyes, and told him to go wash in the pool of Siloam. In Mark Chapter 10:52, Jesus doesn't touch blind Bartimaeus' eyes, He just speaks to him and says, "Go, your faith has healed you," and immediately he received his sight. In Matthew Chapter 20, two blind men are following Jesus and, after some time, He finally turns to them and asked them, "What do you want me to do for you?"

They said, "We want to see." This time Jesus didn't spit on the ground and He didn't use mud. He simply touched their eyes and immediately they regained their sight and followed Him. Here we see three different instances where Jesus healed the blind, but He never did it the same way. Stop looking for God to do it the same way He did it the last time. The miracle isn't attached to the method; the miracle is connected to the miracle worker.

He promises to make all things new, but the "new" can come in various different forms. I'm not sure how God is going to create your "new," but I do know for a fact that if you keep believing and trusting in Him, He will do just that. A trick of the enemy is to derail us by making us focus on the passed time. Many people count the years and months that have passed by and they make the mistake of believing that God is no longer going to answer their prayers. They believe that maybe they're disqualified because of the Chronos time, and so they fall out of faith. At these points of wavering faith, it's important to remind yourself that God moves on Kairos time. Don't let doubt take you out of your game or snatch your destiny away. You were derailed, not denied. You are still under a covenant, and in case you haven't noticed, God does not break covenants. He promises to give us beauty for ashes.

As I was studying the various examples of "new" in the kingdom of God, I learned that it can come about in various ways, including by restoration, repositioning, reconciling, renaming, or resurrecting. Let's take a moment to discuss the various ways that "new" can come about in your life. I believe that by examining these five Rs and some biblical passages that support these thoughts, you will receive new revelation on what God has and is doing in your life. Remember that no two blessings are the same.

Focus on the creative power of God in making new blessings, grace, and beginnings in the lives of His children. God is so committed to the "new" that He Himself became a new life, a walking human being that was fully God and fully man, just to save the world from death. He is a genius, no doubt!

Restoration

The act of restoring means to renew or to put back to a former state. To illustrate this, God took me to the story of the man with the withered hand in Mark Chapter 3. One Sabbath day, Jesus walked into a synagogue and saw a man with a withered hand. The religious leaders asked Jesus if it was lawful to heal on the Sabbath, and He responded, "Which one of you who has a sheep, if it falls into a pit on the Sabbath, will not take hold of it and lift it out? Of how much more value is a man than a sheep! So it is lawful to do good on the Sabbath." He called the man to the front of the church and asked him to stretch out his hand. Now I can imagine the man wanting to be healed, but why would Jesus want him to stretch his hand out in front of the whole church? If he did that, then everyone would know that his hand was withered. Why couldn't he just keep his condition hidden away in his pocket as he had been doing for years now? Why did he have to stand up in front of the entire synagogue and show everyone?

As long as he was able to keep his hand hidden away, even though people may not have known what he was dealing with, and that kept him from the public shame and embarrassment, he would have had to hide this for the rest of his life. Jesus gave him the opportunity to be made whole. God told me, "I cannot heal what you are afraid to reveal." As long as we are hiding our withered hands in our pockets and pretending like we don't have issues, God cannot truly get the glory out of our lives. Remember we were created for His glory and good pleasure. *You are worthy, our Lord and God, to receive glory and honor and power, for you created all things, and by your will they were created and have their being* (Rev. 4:11). The man stretched out his hand, and it was restored to resemble his good hand.

We don't know if this man's hand had been hurt in an accident or if the man was born that way. Regardless, a healed hand was a new thing to this guy. Can you imagine walking around your entire life, or just one year of your life, with a withered hand? I imagine it being old, dry, limp, paralyzed, wrinkled, and unable to function properly. He may not have even had feeling in that hand. This man had probably never threw a football or dunked a basketball with his withered hand. He wouldn't have been able to shake hands with anyone, and he was probably quite embarrassed of it. He and his family probably referred to it as the "bad hand," writing it off as worthless. You know how this goes. How many times do we hear people say, "That's the bad child," or "You know they're the bad seed"? It's human nature to label people and things as they appear to be, not as they were created to be. It was a worthless limb. Imagine him trying to talk to a woman and wanting to ask her out on a date. He probably kept that withered hand in his pocket afraid that she'd reject him at the sight of it. On that Sabbath day, however, Jesus brought hope into that synagogue. He brought with Him the promise of newness and of restoration.

Have you ever been rejected because of something undesirable… a bruise, speech problem, poor grades, bad past? What if one day someone came into your life and said they wanted to heal that withered area? That day has come my friend… except Jesus is not a man and all He wants is your trust and honor.

Jesus is in the business of restoring our withered and broken areas, and when He does, there is no trace of the "less than" state that we were in before. The scripture says that the man's hand was restored to resemble the other, meaning his good hand. Restored items do not resemble what existed prior to the restoration. A restored house does not look like the one underneath the new paint, floors, windows, and fixtures. Restoration is a form of a new beginning that comes with knowing Christ. Jesus doesn't care who's around when He gets ready to restore us either. As we learn in this miracle story, He doesn't mind breaking the rules, and He certainly doesn't mind overriding earthly authorities to bless his people.

One last thing: *they* don't have to like you for God to bless you! He's going to bless you in the presence of your enemies. Just stay faithful!

Take a moment and write down some areas in your life that need restoration. Write them down, and then pray.

_____

_____

_____

_____

_____

_____

Restoration Prayer:

Lord in your Word you say, "For I will restore health to you, and your wounds I will heal," (Jer. 30:17). Father God, I am asking that you touch the areas above, and restore them in the name of Jesus Christ. I do not want to continue operating within those areas as they are now. I decree and declare that there is nothing missing, broken, or lacking, and I will believe that you have released restoration until I see it manifest in the natural. You promised to make all things new, and I thank you for keeping your promises to me. I thank you and I praise you, in Jesus' name, amen.

Repositioning

Has there ever been a time or moment in your life when you experienced a sudden upgrade, move, promotion, or change in status or tax bracket? If so, you most likely experienced a spiritual repositioning. When we experience a repositioning in Christ, the Lord literally changes our position or status. We see this play out in Luke 1. The angel Gabriel appeared to Mary, a virgin married to Joseph. First he let her know that she was favored and that the Lord was with her. Then, he told her that since she was favored, God selected her to carry His very own child, Jesus the Messiah. Gabriel then shared with Mary that she would be impregnated by the Holy Spirit and informed her that her cousin Elizabeth, who was previously barren, would also be having a child in a few months. It would seem that in a blink of an eye, Mary went from being an unknown, engaged woman to the mother of the world's savior. In the spiritual world however, we know from Jeremiah 29:11 that God knew Mary before she was even formed. Not only did He know her, but He knew His purposes for her. It often takes the natural world decades to catch up with the spiritual, and so to redeem the time, God often repositions His children physically, spiritually, and publically. When this happens, we are positioned to carry out the destiny that He has for us. Repositioning is one of the exciting ways that we can expect God's "new" to manifest after a destiny derailment.

Before we move on, I want you to notice something. Mary had to also participate and authorize God's plan to reposition her. After hearing God's grand plans for her life, Mary asked the Angel Gabriel, "How can this be, since I do not know a man?" (Luke 1:34). He told her that the Holy Spirit would impregnate her. At this point, Mary was probably thinking all types of stuff, including how embarrassing it would be to walk around telling people that she was a pregnant virgin. When we hear something that sounds impossible, the first emotion that tries to grip us is fear. Gabriel affirmed her and said, "For with God nothing will be impossible." Mary's next response changed the course of her life and ours. She said, "Let it be to me according to your word." Mary's "yes" authorized God to bless her, to reposition her, and to redeem the time for all of God's chosen people.

Do you believe that God is in the process of repositioning you? Pray for insight, below.

Repositioning Prayer:

God, I thank you for repositioning me out of the kingdom of darkness into the kingdom of light. I surrender to your sovereign will over my life. I pray that you make me sensitive to your Holy Spirit so that I can discern when you are repositioning me spiritually, geographically, or socially so that I live your will. For with you, I know that nothing is impossible. I thank you Lord. In Jesus' name, amen.

Relocation

Similar to repositioning, God sometimes relocates us to create "new" in our lives or a new life altogether. To relocate means to establish in a new place. Have there been times in your life when you needed to be established in a new place? There are several stories about God relocating His chosen ones so that they could fulfill their destinies in Christ—both modern-day stories and biblical ones. Noah had to relocate from land to an ark. Abram and Sarai located from Haran, when they received word from God to *"Go from your country and your kindred and your father's house to the land that I will show you. And I will make of you a great nation, and I will bless you and make your name great, so that you will be a blessing. I will bless those who bless you, and him who dishonors you I will curse, and in you all the families of the earth shall be blessed (Gen. 12:1-3)."* God called Moses to help the Israelites relocate from Egypt to a promised land, and Esther had to relocate to the king's palace to be discovered and crowned queen. At the time of Jesus' birth, even Mary and Joseph had to relocate from Bethlehem to Egypt because the reigning King Herod wanted to kill baby Jesus.

God will relocate us to protect us, to speak with us, to isolate and mature us, and to prepare us for the destiny that He has for us. Sometimes, in that place of relocation, He promises us new territory, as He did with the Israelites and with Abraham. Often, the new and unfamiliar of your relocation can seem like a destiny derailment in itself. If God has relocated you to unfamiliar territory, there is a reason. The key is to view it as a blessing and to go deeper to determine His purpose during your time there. There is always a purpose when God does something new, especially isolation through relocation. If there have been times in your life when God relocated you, identify the lessons that you learned in those places.

If the Lord has orchestrated a relocation in your life, and you are still in that place, the prayer below is for you.

Relocation Prayer:

Heavenly Father, I may not know what you're doing, but I trust you. I come to you in the name of your Son Jesus Christ asking you for a complete revelation regarding this relocation. Lord, what are you seeking to teach me? How are you seeking to prune me? What do you want me to see about you and to see about me? Please, HOLY SPIRIT, lead me to the truth regarding this relocation and allow me to catch every lesson intended for me to receive in this place. Thank you, Lord, for making all things new! In Jesus' name, amen.

Reconciliation

Therefore, if anyone is in Christ, the new creation has come: The old has gone, the new is here! All this is from God, who reconciled us to himself through Christ and gave us the ministry of reconciliation: that God was

reconciling the world to himself in Christ, not counting people's sins against them. And he has committed to us the message of reconciliation. We are therefore Christ's ambassadors, as though God were making his appeal through us. We implore you on Christ's behalf: Be reconciled to God. God made him who had no sin to be sin for us, so that in him we might become the righteousness of God.
2 Corinthians 5:17-19

To reconcile means to restore to friendship or harmony. The language and concept of "reconciliation" can be confusing to understand; why in the world you would need to be reconciled or restored to harmony with God? All humans do. You see, even before the derailment that may have caused you to go off track, as a human being, you already needed to be reconciled with God. This is because of the fall of humanity that took place in the Garden of Eden with Adam and Eve. Their disobedience of God forever placed humankind outside of a harmonious relationship with Him. In the Old Testament, Israelites attempted to atone for this by offering sacrifices. Thankfully, God realized that we, as humans, needed one sacrifice and one act that would reconcile us to Him once and for all. That One was Jesus Christ. Nothing or no one else was sufficient. Today, those who are in Christ are also invited by God to become a part of His world reconciliation plan.

In 2 Corinthians 5:18, the Greek word used for reconciled literally means to exchange or to restore to divine favor or atonement. We were all reconciled to Christ at the point of salvation, but not only that, the Bible tells us that we each have the ministry of reconciliation. This is great news—if you have yet to figure out a mission for your life—the Word tells us that after we were reconciled to Christ, He gave us that same duty, to become His ambassadors, reconciling unbelievers to Him. We are made new through this reconciliation, and when we fall off track, our repentance, paired with the blood of Christ, continuously reconciles us back to divine favor. Don't allow a derailment to keep you from the divine favor, the new being in Christ that you have become. You are reconciled—atoned of your sins, and you now have a duty to continue living so that others can be reconciled and made new as well. Extend your hand in solidarity, offer your shoulder to cry on.

You were made new and now others will need you to fully embrace that so that you can pull them up. Christ leveled the playing field for each of us by wiping everyone's slates clean. He didn't just do this once; he wipes our slates clean over and over again, as we repent for the sins that we commit daily. He has never-ending grace and there is enough for you. Christ is our superhero who died on the cross and was resurrected three days later so that we could be reconciled to Him. Reconciliation in the kingdom of God is synonymous with "new."

Reconciliation Prayer:

God, thank you for reconciling me to you through Christ Jesus. Increase my faith so that I can fully accept the grace you've given me despite anything that I've done. I thank you Lord for loving me so much that you've made me one with you. In Jesus' name, amen.

Renaming

In the Bible, God often gave people new names to signify their renewed purpose and a change in direction on their destiny paths. Jesus told Simon that his name would be "Peter". Peter means "rock," and in Matthew 16:18, Jesus told him, "On this rock, I will build my church." Jesus did just that—Peter went on to preach the sermon at Pentecost, where 3,000 people received Christ. God changed Abram and Sarai's names to Abraham and Sarah to signify God's promise to make Abraham the father of many nations. In the book of Acts, Saul, who was previously a murderer of Christians, became Paul, the great apostle who would bring the message of salvation to the Gentiles and write thirteen of the twenty-six books of the New Testament.[5] In our modern culture, often name changes occur for societal or educational purposes. New wives go from Ms. Maiden Name to Mrs. Married Name; a student who completes a certain amount of school can be referred to as Dr., MBA, MFA. In God's eyes, we go from being sinners to saints once we accept Christ.

However, most importantly, our names change to son or daughter of God. What's amazing about this is that when we get derailed, He doesn't change our names back to sinners. No, we are still saints! We are still sons and still daughters of Christ.

You may have been known as something in your former years—perhaps a thief, adulterer, liar—but now, you are none of those things. God calls you a redeemed saint. He has renamed you according to your new identity. Whenever our names change, there is something new happening. Has God made you new, and changed your name or title. How people see you now is an indication of this change.

What are some of the new names that you have in Christ?

_____

_____

_____

_____

_____

Renaming Prayer:

Lord, help me to fully understand, accept, and live according to my new identity in you. In the name of Jesus, please raise a hedge of protection around my mind so that I do not fall victim to the enemy's attempted identity theft of me. God, I thank you for renaming me. Show me how to live as your ambassador and show me how to serve you in spirit and in truth, in Word and in deed, according to my identity in you. Thank you Father. In Jesus' name, amen.

Resurrection

In the Gospel of John Chapter 11, we read about the raising of Lazarus, which was the final display of miracles in a series of Jesus miracles. These extraordinary acts prove without a shadow of a doubt that He is the Messiah. This particular miracle not only served as a sign of what was to come in Christ's own life, but that He Himself is the giver of life. He is the author of new. Jesus raised Lazarus from the dead after he was in the grave for four days. Jesus waited until Lazarus was good and dead to perform this miracle just so that people in Lazarus' community would believe in Jesus. He wanted to demonstrate to everyone in attendance, all the people in Lazarus' town, and all who would hear and read about this miracle that death is no match for Him. He has the power to create new life—that being associated with Him is all we need to experience resurrection and renewal. Jesus still does this today.

In my own personal life, I truly thought my career was dead. It had been in the grave for months. The requests to perform stopped. I wasn't on the road or the ministry circuit like I had grown accustomed to. It's safe to say that things were looking quite dead for me. But God had a different plan. Just like He did with Lazarus, Jesus waited until things looked really bad and then He changed the course of my life, picked up my derailed train car, and put me back on track. I experienced a resurrection like I would have never imagined. Keep reading. In the final chapter of this book, I'm going to share just how God can and will use a resurrection of life and purpose to make all things new.

Resurrection Prayer:

Jesus, I don't need any more proof that you are able to resurrect life and make all things new. God, resurrect every dead thing that I will need for my destiny. In Jesus' name, Amen.

Reflection: *All Things New*

Repeat this: *He makes all things new. He makes all things new. He makes all things new.* Just by being a child of God, that is a promise that you can take to the bank or to the grave. If something in your life seems to have met the grave, put your trust in the Lord, who makes all things new. Your derailment was not the end of you. I'm excited for your future. I'm not sure how God will or has done it for you—whether you experienced a resurrection, a renaming, or reconciliation, but I know that He has done it. Yes, I say HAS, because Ephesians 1:3 says that He has already released your blessings. So are you ready for all things to be made new in your life? Are you ready for your revived purposed, your renewed strength, your rekindled hope?

In the space below, write a little note to yourself telling yourself and God what NEW THINGS you're looking forward to.

_____

_____

_____

_____

_____

Chapter 10: *Dear Future Me*

Dear Future Me,
You had every reason to give up, but instead, you got up.
You made up your mind that one season of your life will not define
your lifetime. Your faith has been tested and proven, and now it's time
to focus on the future.

- James Fortune

On May 5, 2015, I received a disturbing text message from my brother. During this time, I was still in the thick of family violence therapy and also enrolled in personal one-on-one life coaching—still out of the public eye and trying to rebuild. Needless to say, I didn't want or need any more bad news. He told me that a longtime friend, the daughter of a local pastor had been in a horrible accident. I had known her for what seemed like forever. Her mom and my dad both pastor churches in Houston. My brother was a musician at her mom's church. Our families had ties, and this news shook me to my bones. He told me that her injuries were severe, and that she wasn't expected to live.

It was a Tuesday evening, and she was driving northbound on I-59 in Houston, exiting the Richmond ramp, and she saw bright lights coming directly towards her. Panic overwhelmed her as she thought she was driving in the wrong direction. Before she could fully come up with a plan to escape the inevitable, the drunk driver, coming straight towards her windshield, hit her head on. I imagine that her life flashed before her eyes as she called out the name of Jesus. The intensity of the pain magnified. After being unconscious for a while, she woke up to chaos around her, red and blue lights, and the Jaws of Life cutting her out of her vehicle. An ambulance transported her to the hospital, but one of the officers on the scene was in such shock and disbelief at the state of her body that he pronounced her Dead on Arrival when he couldn't find a pulse. They transported her to the hospital. Remember when I told you that Jesus resurrected life? Well, in the emergency room, the doctors were able to resuscitate her. She made it, and in the eyes of the doctors she literally went from death to life.

I went to visit my friend three days later. During that time, I just wanted to be there for her, and since I was not ministering in public, I believe that being with her during her recovery actually ministered to me. It's funny how when you think you're helping someone out but being there in the midst of their storm actually helps you. I began to share my heart with her and encourage her as she fought for her future, which, she was determined, did not include being tied to a hospital bed for the rest of her life.

During this time, it was less than a year after my derailment, and I was still soaking in shame and embarrassment. I had moments when I didn't want to leave the house and I didn't want to talk to anyone. However, the timing of it all was really wild. She and I had a familiarity and a common bond. We could relate to each other without judgement, without shame, and without fear of being vulnerable. I could not imagine being in her shoes. Her fight showed me that things could be worse. Seeing her survive the worst derailment of her life made me want to embrace every day of my life and the future that God still was giving me. I thought I had it bad, but this woman didn't deserve this. She didn't ask for it, and she didn't do anything wrong to be in the hospital fighting for a normal life. Instead of complaining about how unfair this was and even allowing her mind to drift into a negative space, I watched as she maintained a positive outlook on life. She truly inspired me to fight just the way she was fighting. She fought with courage and confidence. It made me say and believe, *Dear Future Me, I'm ready for you.*

Her name is Rhaquele, and watching her fight for her life from a hospital bed gave me a new perspective on all of the possibilities I had now that I'd been given a second chance. As the weeks and months passed, I continued to watch her fight for a normal life during intense physical therapy treatments. After that accident, although she made it out alive, her life of normalcy as she knew it had ended. She had to learn to walk and speak properly again. In the blink of an eye, Rhaquele went from being independent to reliant on others just to help her with basic day-to-day functions. The doctors thought she'd never walk again, but it wasn't long before she began taking steps. It was great to have a friend who didn't judge me, and I guess she felt the same. We were both in really sensitive spaces and we needed a real friend—someone solid who would push us through the hardest times of our lives. God spared Rhaquele's life, and afterwards, she went through a pruning season, similar to what I experienced, where He removed people who weren't supposed to be there while bringing those into her life who did belong.

During this time, I was still working through my own issues. I was going through the process of taking accountability for my actions and not ever wanting to repeat my past mistakes. I was also rekindling the relationship with my children, and my time was committed to them. In between taking them out on daddy-daughter dates and going to therapy sessions, I prayed a lot, wrote material that would end up on my album, and visited Rhaquele as she took one baby step after the next to begin walking again. She and I became a part of each other's Comeback Circle, and it was cool, because we could share our small victories with one another. When she had a painless night of rest or when I received a new mental revelation that seemed to push me forward, we celebrated. I learned the importance of celebrating small wins, and I was soaking in every lesson my therapist was teaching. Having a friend like Rhaquele there during this time was priceless. As I'm writing this, I am reminded of an earlier lesson that I shared in this book: that God won't just put anyone in our circles, but He will put in the right ones. She was exactly who I needed.

When I started working on the *Dear Future Me* album, God had started breaking down the internal issues within me, and I could see things clearly. I was newly divorced, and still harbored some anger. I wrote the album from my heart and was extremely excited to begin recording in early 2016. I called my producer, Ayron Lewis, who had produced so many songs for me and as soon as we started working, it was like old times. Once again, God began to repurpose my past pain into encouraging lyrics. With Ayron's talent, things simply fell into place.

By the time we finished the album, and 2017 came around, I had been out of the public eye for two and a half years. My children and I had created a new normal where they visited with me several times a week. We took trips to the beach, the gym, and other places that we could enjoy together. I accompanied my daughters at cheerleading, karate, and basketball games, and we worked through the pain that we were all feeling as well as the new family dynamics. Work was still slow and I had spent over a year in the studio pouring my heart into my album. The two years of counseling had made me see me for me. The façade was rolled away. The pretentiousness and saving public face had been longed ripped away too. In the studio, just like on my therapist's couch, I was able to reveal my true feelings. Over time, I saw me grow. The anger turned to sadness. The sadness turned to acceptance. The acceptance turned to coping. And the coping turned to living. With the release of *Dear Future Me,* I was hoping to thrive in my purpose again. I penned "My Letter," the same one you read at the beginning of this chapter, to capture that moment in time. I was ready. *Finally,* I thought, *I've dealt with the Past Me. And now, I'm ready to meet the Future Me.*

I worked with Gina Miller, a true blessing to my life, who is the VP of my record label, Entertainment One, to develop a marketing strategy for the album, yet we didn't know what to expect. I felt like a new artist all over again. I'd been off of social media and slowly beginning to engage with the public again. Releasing *Dear Future Me* bought up feelings of fear that I hadn't experienced in a really long time. In my mind, I thought that people had forgotten about me. *Perhaps they have written me off,* I often told myself. I knew the Word of God, and I had faith despite any indication, except my gut, that this album would perform well. I knew that I had sincerely repented. I believed that God could put my life and my purpose back on track. I had been diligent in my work, and I poured my heart and soul—my entire truth—into that album. My future was calling. I could no longer remain trapped in a derailment—off course in a season in time that attempted to define my life. I could no longer stay in that place. I was sure that *Dear Future Me* would bless people, and that just like in the past, the songs on the album were not designed to only minister to me, but they had the potential to help anyone who heard them, others who'd experienced a derailment. Part of the marketing strategy for the record was to presell the album for two months prior to the official release date of June 23, 2017. As the presale date creeped closer, I decided that I would stop worrying. **"If you're going to worry about it, don't pray about it!"** Right? That's what I told myself.

I soon realized God planned an encore with *Dear Future Me.* We were basing the perceptibility of the album and me as an artist on the sales of course. I remember when we put it up for pre-order in April, and Paul at Entertainment One called to share the early numbers with us. If you can imagine, I was holding my breath as he shared the news.

"James, it looks like you never left! The numbers are higher than any of your other albums."

I was stunned. Prior to this moment, I had faith mixed with fear. We had no clue how people were going to respond. The "buzz" was quiet. The media was quiet. Social media was quiet. We didn't know how people were going to respond. It was like the scripture in 2 Kings 6, when Elisha prayed for God to open the young man's eyes, and when He did, there was a great army–more than the opposing side. God showed me through the release of *Dear Future Me* that there were more people with me than who were against me. More importantly, God showed me that He still loved me and He still trusted me with my gifts and His people.

It was a blessing and a great sign. It was a relief and a confirmation that God was still with me. It confirmed what my Dad had said, that "they" can take my things, but they couldn't take my gift. It's one thing to hear and see people say that they support you, but for me to find success in pre-orders, it showed that people still cared enough to actually spend the money buying the album. I didn't know that people were truly behind me. When we go through something bad, and, especially when we're to blame, it's easy to feel like we're all alone and that no one cares or wants to support any more. But *Dear Future Me* disproved this false theory that I had about my life. One record exec from another label called and said, "James I really respect you because you could have come out with an album and acted like nothing ever happened, but you put this album together and allowed it to show your vulnerability. It makes me respect you even more." I also believe that my transparency helped people move past what happen. I was real, and I think my fans and supporters were able to hear my heart and forgive me for things that I had done.

Dear Future Me ended up reaching #1 on the Billboard charts, and it received three nominations at the Stellar Gospel Music Awards. At the time of me writing this book, it's almost a year later. **I am on my first major tour, over 50-cities, since that derailment.** I am truly free. I have truly met my Future Me, and to top things off, my family has begun to feel like a cohesive unit again.

In late 2017, I realized that Rhaquele was the missing piece to my puzzle. After over a decade of friendship, working together, years of knowing each other, fighting through our hardest times together and building an authentic friendship, I proposed to her at Houston's restaurant in Houston, Texas during dinner. I was super nervous, but I had no doubt that God sent her to me and she was my wife.

We married in a private ceremony in Mexico. The only attendees were her mom, my mom and her husband, Pastor Armond Brown, and my sister Sherry and her husband, Cortez. Rhaquele's mom, who is a pastor, presided over the ceremony. Depending on when you read this book, she and I may still be newlyweds. Perhaps I am still on the biggest tour of my life, and God is still pushing my train forward toward my destiny.

I wrestled back and forth with whether or not to include this part in the book. We didn't make a big announcement on social media, nor did I arrange cameras, a reality television show, or paparazzi to follow us around. I honestly had to be convinced to share the details of my relationship with Rhaquele with my readers. At the end of the day, however, I was convinced to reveal this intimate and honest aspect of my life to encourage everyone who's been derailed. As you've read from the previous pages, it's so easy to believe that life can never be the same or better than it was prior to making mistakes or falling off course. Too many of us flawed believers who have made life-altering mistakes walk around each day with a dark cloud of doom believing the lie that we somehow have disqualified ourselves for God's blessings. Yes, I messed up. I messed up big time, and yet I was not disqualified for success, restoration, redemption, and love. Regardless of any mistakes that we make, our repentance and change of heart are what matters most to God. He is not looking for perfection from you or me. He just wants progress. Why would a perfect God need or expect perfect children? I wake up every day in awe with what God has done. I look at my new wife and I am more blown away as I consider the way God not only restored me, but how He resurrected and restored her and allowed us to reconnect. Whatever you can imagine for your life is nothing compared to what God wants to do. As I've been on tour traveling from city-to-city, ministering to bigger crowds than ever before, I feel the presence of God. I feel the purpose of God, and I see the power of God.

Throughout this process, I've realized that a trick of the enemy is to make us believe that we will forever be derailed. He wants us to believe that one bad decision or circumstance has cost us our destiny. He wants us to believe that we are forever failures. My hope and prayer is that God will use this book and my life to encourage you to welcome your future self and accept that God most definitely has a future for you… regardless of what you've been through.

A derailed train does not stay off track. In fact, over the years, there have been so many derailments and train accidents that engineers have actually begun to invent systems to prevent train derailments. Once I learned about some of the newer technology, I realized that we can do this as well. We too can establish systems to prevent us from going totally off track. If you have certain triggers, people, or circumstances that seem to disrupt you from purpose, how can you implement systems to prevent them from causing derailments to your destiny? In the world of railroads, there is a technology called Positive Train Control (PTC), which is an advanced system designed to automatically stop a train before certain accidents occur. Do you remember how I mentioned that derailments and speed are two of the most common causes of train crashes? Well, The PTC system was designed to prevent train-to-train collisions, derailments caused by excessive speed, and other common issues. This is great news. Take this as your cue that you too can put in place systems to prevent derailments.

Many people walk around with the idea that they have to be subject to their thoughts, environment, toxic family members, and other components that cause derailments. This is not true. God has given us authority in Christ to take control of our lives to ensure that we are not susceptible to the devil's schemes.

No temptation has overtaken you except what is common to mankind. And God is faithful; he will not let you be tempted beyond what you can bear. But when you are tempted, he will also provide a way out so that you can endure it.

1 Corinthians 10:13

You are not what you went through. What you went through doesn't define you. What you went through has prepared you for what God has already set aside for you. You cannot erase what you've been through nor can you erase what others have done to you, but you can make a decision today to let it go. You can make a decision to meet the Future You and walk into the destiny that God has designed for you. Your destiny is no longer derailed.

Reflection: *Dear Future Me*

Thank you for reading *Destiny Derailed*. This has been a journey, and you probably have tons of thoughts now. I've shared some intimate parts of my life as well as several biblical and therapeutic tools that helped me get through. Before the final reflection activity below, I want to leave you with two important takeaways. First, as you read throughout this book, therapy was a major component of my healing. Although many people look down on professional counseling and therapy, I know that it can and is the game changer for many people. Do not hesitate to speak with a professional about the mental, physical, spiritual, and emotional pain you've experienced. Equally as important is the forgiveness factor. Before meeting the Future You, you have to forgive yourself, forgive those who hurt you, and embrace the truth that God has forgiven you.

Below, take a moment to reflect on your biggest takeaways from this book. When you finish, be sure to tell more people about *Destiny Derailed*. Together we can help a generation get back on track after their biggest setbacks.

My biggest takeaways are:

_____

_____

_____

_____

CONNECT WITH **JAMES**!

MrJamesFortune

MrJamesFortune

The Official James Fortune

References

1. http://www.independent.co.uk/news/world/europe/austria-train-crash-latest-updates-dead-injured-niklasdorf-rail-police-emergency-a8206706.html

2. https://www.purdue.edu/discoverypark/nextrans/assets/pdfs/Integrating%20Hazardous%20Materials%20Transportation%20Safety%20Risk%20Management%20Framework.pdf

3. https://www.psychologytoday.com/blog/talking-about-men/201702/mens-mental-health-silent-crisis

4. https://ideas.ted.com/why-rejection-hurts-so-much-and-what-to-do-about-it/

5. Some scholars debate this, however, it is most commonly believed that Paul is the author of thirteen books of the bible.

About the Author

James Fortune's power when it comes to spreading the Gospel through song is his ability to be transparent and feature life scenarios as the centerpiece of his songwriting. His gifted pen, song arrangements, and vocal delivery, with collaborative assists from his choir FIYA, provides more than repetitious affirmations of overcoming the storm. Instead his songs lyrically strip down life's lemons with intentions to make the listener stronger while guiding them through the journey of faith, forgiveness, and healing. It's a genuine offering that stems from the influence of Kirk Franklin and is further rooted in Fortune's mission to "advance the Kingdom."

Since the music ministry's 2004 debut, "You Survived," James Fortune and FIYA have gone on to record and release *The Transformation (2007), Encore (2010), Identity and Grace Gift (both released in 2012), Dear Future Me (2017)* and *The Collection(2018)*, which fuse elements of hip-hop beats with uplifting lyrical material- a knockout combo that captures and pulls the listener in, providing them with the spiritual fuel they may not even have known was needed. It's truly a heart and reality sentiment when it comes to Fortune's musical testimony.

His lyrics reflect the life that Fortune has lived in a two-dimensional way, in both cause and effect. About 10 years ago, following the release of his debut record, the father of four was homeless. Admittedly ashamed, he kept his living situation and battles a secret. It was during this time that he turned to his God-given talent and began to write, and birthed "I Trust You" while living in a motel room. The single, created during one of Fortune's darkest times, went on to become number one in the country for 29 consecutive weeks—a streak that was unprecedented for a gospel song.

Every soldier has a testimony. It's that war wound that proves you've been tested in the past —and may still be in a storm—but with faith in God, you're growing beyond it and getting through. Today, as an artist, man, and father, James Fortune wears his wounds for all to see, offering his life as a testimony and a representation of self-forgiveness, moving forward, and embracing life with a firm belief that through God and Faith, we ALL have a future.